D1489855

MARRIA(

OF

BEDFORD COUNTY, VIRGINIA

1755-1800

Compiled by

Earle S. Dennis and Jane E. Smith

REPRINTED WITH

Bedford County, Virginia:
Index of Wills, From 1754 to 1830

Edited by Rowland D. Buford

CLEARFIELD

Marriage Bonds of Bedford County, Virginia
Originally Published
Bedford, Virginia, 1932
Reprinted in an Improved Format
Genealogical Publishing Co., Inc.
Baltimore, 1975

Bedford County, Virginia: Index of Wills
Originally Published 1917
Reprinted
Genealogical Publishing Co., Inc.
Baltimore, 1964

Reprinted in a Combined Edition
Genealogical Publishing Co.
Baltimore, Maryland
1976, 1981, 1989

Reprinted for
Clearfield Company by
Genealogical Publishing Co.
Baltimore, Maryland
2004, 2007

Library of Congress Catalogue Card Number 75-4010
ISBN-13: 978-0-8063-0669-8
ISBN-10: 0-8063-0669-6

Made in the United States of America

MARRIAGE BONDS

OF

BEDFORD COUNTY, VIRGINIA

1755—1800

WILLIAM AUSTIN and ESTHER ALEXANDER, January 23, 1781. Robert Alexander,
   surety.

RICHARD ADAMS and ELIZABETH PRUITT, September 12, 1781. Robert Pruitt,
   surety.

RICHARD AUSTIN and FANNY NEAL, April 13, 1793. John Pate, surety. Consent
   of Zachariah Neal.

ROBERT ARMSTRONG and JANE McELWAINE, August 23, 1784. Saml. McElwaine,
   surety.

JAMES ADAMS, batchelor, and MARY IRVINE, spinster, both of this County,
   March 4, 1776. James McMurray, surety. Consent of David Irvine,
   father of Mary.

THOMAS AUSTIN and NANCY NORTH, December 15, 1788. John North, surety.
   Consent of Abram North, father of Nancy.

WILLIAM ANDERSON and SALLY EARLY, December 23, 1783. David Jones, surety.
   Consent of James Callaway, the guardian of Sally.

JOSIAH ASHURST and REBECKAH KENNEDY, July 25, 1793. Samuel Hatcher, surety.

SAMUEL AYERS and BETSEY RICHARDSON, October 27, 1794. John Cundiff, surety.

LEROY APSHEAR, batchelor, and ELIZABETH BRADLEY, spinster, October 24, 1769.
   William Bradley, surety.

JOHN ANDERSON, batchelor, and ANN BUTLER, widow, June 22, 1772. John Hook,
   surety.

MARK ANTHONY and EMELIA LEFTWICH, December 12, 1799. John Anthony, surety.
   Consent of Thos. Leftwich, the father of Emelia.

BARNABAS ARTHER, batchelor, and MARTHA TALBOT, spinster, May 26, 1755.
   William Arther, surety.

ROBERT ARMISTEAD of Gloucester County, and SUSANNA MORRIS, February 12, 1778.
   William Armistead, surety. Consent of Saml. Morris, father of
   Susanna.

ELISHA ADAMS and FRANKY HUDNALL, February 4, 1783. William Adams, surety.
   Consent of W. Hudnall, father of Franky.

WILLIAM ANGLEA and SARAH MITCHELL, April 5, 1797. John Hancock, surety.
   Consent of Beelender Ross.

THOMAS ADAMS and BETSEY ADAMS, January 28, 1799. George Thomas, surety.
   Consent of William Adams, father of Betsey.

GEORGE ASBURY and MARY HATCHER, May 24, 1785. Edmund Winston, surety. Consent of Bengeman Hatcher, father of Mary.

WILLIAM ARTHUR and JOANNA ARTHUR, August 14, 1787. Boice Eidson, surety. Consent of Thomas Arthur, the father of Joanna; and consent of Gross Scruggs for the marriage of William.

JOHN AUSTIN and SALLY AUSTIN, March 24, 1784. William Austin, surety.

JESSE ANDERSON and ELIZABETH JONES, June 21, 1791. Thomas Johnson, surety. Consent of John Jones, father of Elizabeth.

ROBERT ANDERSON, of the County of Henrico, and MARY READ of Bedford County, March 29, 1784. William Read, surety.

RICHARD ANDERSON and HANNAH PAYNE, January 11, 1793. Micajah McCormack, surety. Consent of Sarah Payne, mother of Hannah.

BENJAMIN ARTHUR, batchelor, and ANNE ARTHUR, April 23, 1765. William Arthur, surety.

BENJAMIN ARTHUR and SARAH TERRILL, November 26, 1781. Edward Woodham, surety.

WILLIAM ARTHER, JR. and ELIZABETH DALTON, spinster, June 24, 1762. Gross Scruggs, surety. Consent of Timothe Dalton.

JOSHUA ADKERSON and NANCY GROOMS, September 22, 1800. Jonathan Grooms, surety.

WILLIAM ADAIR and _____RODGERS, January 22, 1781. John Rodgers, surety.

JOSHUA ABSTEN of the County of Pittsylvania, widower, and MARY CARTER, spinster, of Bedford County. May 9, 1782. Austin Carter, surety. Consent of Mary Carter, mother of Mary.

JAMES ANTHONY and ANN TATE, September 29, 1772. Josiah Carter and John Talbot, sureties. Consent of Henry Tate, father of Ann.

MICAJAH ANTHONY and SALLY TATE, August 1, 1792. Jesse Tate, surety.

JAMES ASBERRY and NANCY WRIGHT, November 13, 1792. Tommy Wright, surety. Consent of John Wright, father of Nancy.

EDWARD ALLEN and WINNEY O'DENIEL, June 25, 1787. John O'deniel, surety.

JAMES ALVERSON and MARY ALLIGRE, February 12, 1781. Jesse Moorman, surety. Consent of Mathew Alligre, the father of Mary.

HENRY ADAMS and REBECCA CHAFFIN, December 20, 1791. Stephen Chaffin, surety.

ROBERT ALEXANDER and ANN AUSTIN, March 10, 1774. William Austin, surety.

ANTHONY APPERSON, widower, and SUSANNAH HOLLAND, spinster, May 2, 1765.
William Irvin, surety. Consent of Peter Holland, father of
Susannah.

SAMUEL ADAMS and PATSY WADE, November 25, 1800. Archibald Wade, surety.
Consent of Isaac Wade, father of Patsey.

JOHN ARTHUR and ELIZABETH ADDAMS, November 12, 1785. Thomas Arthur, surety.
Consent of John Addams.

LEWIS ARTHUR and SARAH HATCHER, May 11, 1786. William Haiden, surety.
Certificate from Sarah herself.

THOMAS ALEXANDER and SARAH HUDDLESTON, May 26, 1800. Henry Huddleston,
surety. Consent of Abraham and Mary Slack for the marriage of
"our daughter Sarah Huddleston."

DAVID ARTHUR and MARY MULLENS, March 11, 1793. Thomas Mullens, surety.

PHILIP BUSH and BETSEY HARDWICK, September 21, 1789. Bartlit Woodard,
surety. Consent of John and Elizabeth Hardwick.

SAMUEL BEARD and MARY MITCHELL, September 5, 1778. Robert Mitchell,
surety.

WILLIAM BANISTER and JUDY WEAR, July 23, 1798. Francis Steel, surety.
Consent of Anny Campbell, and also of James Banister.

JARVIS BURDETT and NANCY BILLUPS, November 27, 1786. William Irvine, surety.
Certificate of Nancy that she is of age.

GEORGE BUNCH and HANNAH HIBBS, November 28, 1787. Micajah Stone, surety.
Consent of Isaac Hibbs, father of Hannah.

JAMES BRANCH and FRANCES TERRY, October 9, 1789. James White, surety.
Consent of Polly Terry, mother of Frances.

HUGH BEARD, batchelor, and SARAH McNOD, spinster, October 15, 1765. John
Romain, surety. Certificate of Sarah McKnob, that she is of age.

JAMES BOYD and HANNAH GIBSON, September 8, 1779. William Cunningham,
surety. Certificate of Hannah herself.

JAMES BOYD and JANE STEVENSON, February 25, 1772. William Boyd, surety.

WILLIAM BOYD, widower, and MARTHA WOOD, widow, (prior to 1776, bond to
King George Third, date destroyed). Alexander Boyles, surety.

WILLIAM BOYD and NANCY READ, September 21, 1797. Francis Read, surety.

WILLIAM BOYD and SUSANNA MOODY, September 29, 1800. Thomas Haid, surety.

JOHN BATES and MARY JONES, November 10, 1774. Alexander Gibbs, surety.
Consent: "Mary Jones, daughter of Wm. and Elizabeth Jones, born
1749, 25th Sept., left to the care of Rich'd and Mary Nance,
Grandfather and mother desires with the assent of said Mary Jones
that you will grant John Bates license as they desire to be
joind together in the holy state of Matrimony as we are willing
to declare on oath the above is true age of said Mary Jones".

FREDERICK BOTT and MARTHA WALL, March 8, 1791. George Wall, surety.
Certificate of Martha that she is of age.

JAMES BUNCH and RUTH HIBBS, March 28, 1791. Joseph Hibbs, surety. Consent
of Isaac Hibbs, father of Ruth.

JOSHUA BURNETT and REBECKAH MILTON, July 23, 1792. Thomas Stump, surety.
Consent of Absolem Milton and Ann, parents of Rebeckah.

ABSALOM BURNETT and PATSEY HOWELL, July 23, 1798. Jeremiah Adams, surety.
Consent of Thomas and Mable Burnett, parents of Absalom.

JAMES BRAMBLETT and MILLEY SHREWSBERRY, December 9, 1789. Charles Caffery,
surety. Consent of Nathl. Shrewsberry, father of Milley.

WILLIAM BURNSIDES and BETSEY FRANKEBERGER, December 30, 1799. James Watson,
surety. Consent of William Frankberger, father of Betsey.

AMOS BALLARD and ELIZABETH FEAZLE, July 25, 1794. Cornelius Pate, surety.
Consent of Jacob Feazle, father of Elizabeth.

CHARLES BRIGHT, JR., and SARAH WATSON, February 28, 1798. Jacob Woodward,
surety.

ADAM BEARD and MARGARET MITCHELL, July 29, 1780. Robert Alexander, surety.

JOSIAH BORROW and MARY RIELTY, June 5, 1787. Rush Milam, surety. Consent
of Margret Rielty.

BARTLETT BASHAM and NANCY FARMER, June 28, 1792. Jesse Farmer, surety.
Certificate of Nancy that she is of age.

WILLIAM BARTEE and MARY DABBS, June 25, 1793. Robert Snoddy, surety.
Certificate of David Jones and Robt. Snoddy, showing that "Mary
Dabbs has no father nor guardian in this part of the country
and further that she is of age to act and do for herself".

WILLIAM BRADLEY and JEMIMA COLE, February 12, 1796. John Pool, surety.
Certificate of "Mima" Coal that she is of age and her parents
dead, and that she has no guardian.

PATRICK BUCKNER and MOLLY EASTEP, July 28, 1783. Thomas Logwood, surety.

4

BENJAMIN BLACK and JEAN BOYD, October 1, 1800. Peter Wagoner, surety. Consent of James Boyd.

WILLIAM BOARD and LUCY JORDAN, October 27, 1800. William Jordan, surety.

WILLIAM BUFORD, batchelor and MARY WELCH, spinster, December 15, 1770. Isham Talbot, surety. Consent of Mary Welch, mother of the above named Mary.

REUBEN BROWN and BETSEY McGEHEE, March 25, 1800. David Saunders, surety.

GEORGE BABER and PEGGEY JONES, January 31, 1798. William Halley, surety. Consent of Julus Jones, father of Peggey.

JOHN BARKSDALE and SUSANNA BURNLEY, December 21, 1778. John W. Holt, surety. Consent of Israel Burnly, father of Susanna.

JOSEPH BRIGHT and NANCY TINNERSON, January 20, 1793. James Tinsley and Jesse Crews, sureties.

DAVID BARTON and ELIZABETH McCORMACK, December 22, 1792. Elisha Barton, surety. Consent of Thomas Barton and Sarah Barton; and Mecager and _____ McCormack.

ELISHA BURNETT and ELIZABETH MILTON, February 25, 1799. Absalom Milton, surety.

GEORGE THOMAS BROWN and ELIZABETH BEST, November ___, 1792. Levi Best, surety. Consent of Druzilla Best, mother of Elizabeth.

JESSE BRADLEY and SUSANNA STANDLEY, September 22, 1783. Robert Fitzhugh, surety. Consent of Plesent Standley, father of Susanna.

THOMAS BARTON and JEAN WIGGONTON, December 22, 1788. Joseph Drury, surety. Certificate of Jean Wigenton.

JONATHAN BASHAM and ELIZABETH JONES, March ___, 1786. Jonathan Basham, surety. Consent of William and Elizabeth Basham; and of Vinson and Elizabeth Jhons, parents of Elizabeth.

ABRAHAM BUFORD and SOPHIA LUMPKIN, December 20, 1796. James Otey, surety. Consent of Thomas Lumpkin, father of Sophia; and consent of Henry Buford, father of Abraham.

JAMES BLACK and NANCY RISE, September 22, 1796. George Medley, surety. Consent of Nancy herself.

CALEB BROWNING and BETSEY SINKLER, September 14, 1791. Isaac Sinkler, surety. Consent of Robert Sinkler, the father of Betsey.

LITTLEBERRY BUNDURANT and MARY SCOTT, September 8, 1790. Joel Bundurant, surety. Consent of James Scott.

GEORGE BENTLEY and UNY ADAMS, April 28, 1794. John Candler, surety. Consent of William Adams, father of Uny.

JAMES BLACKLEY and SALLEY JOHNSON, December ___, 1792. Ralph Thomas,
    surety.

JOHN BAUGHN and DOSHA NOELL, October 28, 1799. Thomas Noell, surety.

ELISHA BARTON and SILLER WITT, October 31, 1787. Andrew Tosh, surety.
    Certificate from Lewsiller Witt for license for self.

ISAAC BANISTER and MARY PHILIPS, December 1, 1795. James Banister, surety.

HENRY BAKER and REBECCA PREAS, March 20, 1799. Thomas Preas, surety.
    Consent of Elizabeth Preas, the mother of Rebecca. Witnessed by
    Thomas Preas and Joseph Preas.

JOHN BILBRO and FANNY JONES, November 21, 1800. Thomas Newell, surety.

JOHN BURKS and MARY STEVENS, May 1, 1785. Philip Owens, surety.

WILLIAM BRUCE and NANCY MILAM, October 1, 1795. William Milam, surety.
    Consent of Salley Milam, mother of Nancy. Witnessed by William
    and Adam Milam.

SAMUEL BEST and JANNY UHLE. Date gone. Surety, Jacob Uhle. Consent of
    Mary Uhle, mother of Janny, dated December 4, 1792.

WILLIAM BABER and BITSEY BOBBETE, September 7, 1799. William Bobbet,
    surety.

REUBEN BRAMLETT and SALLY ABSTON, December 7, 1790. Jesse Abston, surety.

PHILIP BURFORD and ELIZABETH GOFF, 22nd of May, 1799. John Goff, surety.
    Consent of Joseph Goff, father of Elizabeth.

ROBERT BURTON and ELIZABETH SINKLER, March 10, 1798. David Sinkler, surety.
    Consent of George Sinkler, father of Elizabeth.

RANDOLPH BOBBETT and NANCY MAYS, December 24, 1792. Elijah Mays, surety.
    Consent of John Mays.

CLEAVERS BARKSDALE, batchelor, and MARY TALBOT, spinster, May 24, 1772.
    John White Holt, surety. Consent of Mathew Talbot, father of
    Mary.

RHODAM BROWN and ELIZABETH ECKOVEY, August 24, 1795. John James, surety.
    Consent of Mathias Eckovey, father of Elizabeth.

HENRY BUFORD and JANE SHERMAN, August 20, 1799. Reuben Hughes, surety.
    Consent of Henry D. Sherman, father of Jane; and consent of
    Herny Buford, father of Henry.

THOMAS BRYANT and MABEL BURNETT, December 11, 1793. Anderson Milton,
    surety. Consent to marry "my daughter", signed by Absalom and
    Ann Milton.

WILLIAM BANISTER, widower, and ANNE HAILE, widow. April 26, 1763. Isham
    Talbot, surety.

EDWARD BRIGHT and MARY ANN GREGORY, July ___, 1778. James Gatewood, surety. Certificate of Mary Ann herself.

THEODORE BUCKHANON and ELIZABETH NIMMO, January 17, 1789. Nathaniel Shrewsbury, surety. Consent of Robert Nimmo, father of Elizabeth.

WILLIAM BOARD and SALLEY MAYSE, May 28, 1792. James Board, Jr., surety. Consent of John and Susanna Mayse, parents of Salley.

WILLIAM BUFORD and ANNEY PATE, October 20, 1791. Cornelius Pate, surety. Consent of Matthew Pate, father of Anney.

JAMES BUFORD, batchelor, and ELIZABETH BRAMLET, spinster, July 14, 1761. Francis Callaway, surety. Consent of said Betty.

WILLIAM BUFORD, JR., and MARTHA HILL LOGWOOD, October 11, 1783. Henry Hall, surety. Consent of Thomas Logwood, father of Martha.

JOHN BRATCHER and NANCEY SHREWSBURY, May 10, 1793. Drewey Shrewsbury, surety. Consent of Nathaniel Shrewsbury, the father of Nancey.

JOHN BLACK and MICHAEL MARSHALL, November 15, 1778. William Marshall, surety. Consent of William Marshall, the father of Michael.

ROBERT BRADFUTE and SARAH IRVINE, February 8, 1777. Arthur Moseley, surety. Consent of Robert Cowan, shows that Sarah Irvine is an orphan of William Irvine.

JOSEPH BURDEN and MARY ECKHOLS, November 9, 1785. Nicholas Keith, surety. Consent of John Eckhols, father of Mary.

DAVID BOOTHE and ELIZABETH NAPIER, April 8, 1785. Charles Donoho, surety. Consent of Ashford Napier, father of Elizabeth.

ADAM BOYER and PATSEY BROWN, October 8, 1796. Thomas Brown, surety.

BENJAMIN BEACHBOARD and ELIZABETH THOMPSON, June 27, 1778. Thomas Daugherty, surety. Certificate of Elizabeth that she is of lawful age.

JOHN BOOTH and TOMSEY THORP, February 4, 1784. George Booth, surety. Consent of William Thorp, father of Tomzey.

WILLIAM BURTON and ELIZABETH MILLS, October 12, 1786. Jesse Reynolds, surety. Certificate of Elizabeth that she is of lawful age.

WILLIAM BROWN and SARAH PAYNE, December 7, 1789. William Payne, surety. Consent of John and Mary Payne.

JOHN BROWN and ANN BURNLEY, January 20, 1775. Joel Burnley, surety. Consent of Israel Burnley, father of Ann.

DANIEL BROWN and POLLY CALLAWAY, August 4, 1781. James Steptoe, surety.

HENRY BROWN and FANNY THOMPSON, January 7, 1792. John Patrick, surety.
Consent of John Thompson, father of Fanny.

RICHARD BROWN and SARAH WOMAX, December 2, 1794. John Folden, surety.
Consent of Sarah Hancock "This is to certify that I, Sarah
Hancock has no objections aginst the maredg that is dependin
betwixt Richard Brown & my Daughter."

JAMES BAILEY and NANCEY BULLOCK, September 27, 1796. Arthur Moseley,
surety. Consent of Hannah Bullock, the mother of Nancy.

JOHN BLACK and JENNY READ, December 29, 1794. Moses Dooley, surety.
Certificate of Francis Reid, father of Jenny, that she is of age.

PETER BOOTH and ELIZABETH BOOTH, December 29, 1783. George Booth, surety.

JOHN BARGHER and CHRISTIANA FRANKLIN, August 27, 1791. John Toughmen,
surety.

RICHARD BURDICK (BURDETT) and POLLEY PAINE, November 27, ____. Thomas
Nicholas, surety. Consent of William Payn, father of Polley,
dated Nov. 27, 1797.

THOMAS BENNETT and ELIZABETH PERRY, April 24, 1784. Thomas Gouge, surety.

JOHN BOOTH and PRUDENCE STAPLES, November 6, 1780. John Staples, surety.
Consent of David Staples. Witnesses Christian Staples, John
Staples, William Staples, and David Staples.

THOMAS BARNES, batchelor, and ELIZABETH CALLAWAY, spinster, September 9,
1766. John Talbot, surety. Consent of James Callaway, father
of Elizabeth.

WILLIAM BATES and ELIZABETH GIBBS, May 13, 1799. David Gibbs, surety.

ALEXANDER BROWN and VILET BARTON, February 20, 1791. Brer Barton, surety.

CHARLES BURRASS and ELIZABETH ALLIGRE, August 2, 1779. William Alligre,
surety. Consent of Mathew and Elizabeth Alligre, parents of
Elizabeth.

GLOVER BAKER and MARY FERRELL, May 19, 1779. David Pagan, surety. Consent
of William Ferrell, father of Mary.

EDWARD BRUSCBANKS and ANNA VAUGHN, March 11, 1797. Benjamin Vaughn, surety.

MOSES BLACKWELL and NANCY BURKS, January 14, 1799. Joseph Holt, surety.
Certificate of Nancy herself.

THOMAS BUNDURANT and PEGGY DRURY, January 23, 1792. Thomas Pullen, surety.

ROBERT BOGGS and MARY VANCE, May 25, 1778. Samuel Beard, surety.
Certificate of said Mary.

PLEASANT BRANCH and JENNY MASTIN, February 14, 1781. Peter Forqueron, Jr.,
surety.

8

JONATHAN BLACKBURN and PRUDENCE BUFORD, November 6, 1797. Henry Buford, surety. Consent of Henry Buford, father of Prudence.

JAMES BRANCH and MARTHA MINOR, April 23, 1792. Edmund Goode and William Minor, sureties.

BENJAMIN BLANKENSHIP and PATIENCE JACKSON, March 19, 1792. Henry Jones, surety. Consent of Able and Hanney Jackson.

SAMUEL BAKER and BETSY TRENT, March 29, 1796. Ob. H. Trent, surety. Consent of Obediah H. Trent, father of Betsey.

HENRY BROOKS and RACHEL FROST, March 23, 1778. John Anderson, surety. Certificate that Rachel is upwards of 21 years.

MICHAEL BOWYER of Campbell County and POLLEY HOWELL, December 27, 1799. John Stevens, surety. Certificate of Polly that she is of age.

SAVAGE BAILEY and FRANKY CRIDDLE, November 2, 1780. Jacob Key, surety.

FREDERICK BOLTZ and KATHRINE MAYBERRY, November 12, 1793. Fred'k Mayberry, surety.

STEPHEN BOARD and LETTICE VAUGHN, March 24, 1800. William Terry, surety.

JULIUS BLACKBURN and ELIZABETH SCRUGGS, January 24, 1785. Henry Buford, surety. Consent of Thomas Scruggs.

THOMAS BURGESS and WINNEY CAUDLE KEY, December 21, 1789. John Key, surety.

ROBERT BAKER and HANNAH FARRELL, April 7, 1781. John Frazier, surety.

WILLIAM BENNETT and SALLY NEAL, March 17, 1797. John Neal, surety.

AMBROSE BRUCE and PATIENCE BRYANT, November 8, 1793. William Bruce, surety. Consent: "This is therefor to sertefi unto you that I Pachence Bryant of Bedford County ar willing that Ambrose Bruce should have my Daughter Nance, as witness my hand.
(Signed) Pachence Bryant and Nance Bryant.
Test, Elijah Bryant."

ABNER BENNETT and ANN JENNINGS, August 7, 1782. Reuben Bennett, surety. Consent of Annah Jennings and Reuben Bennett.

ALEXANDER BURTON and ELIZABETH LEFTWICH, April 12, 1796. Frazier Otey, surety. Consent of W. Leftwich, father of Betsey.

ELIJAH BARTON and ANNA SENTER, January 28, 1792. David Barton, surety. Consent of John and Elizabeth Senter; says Anna is 22 years old.

JOHN BROWN and CONSTANT CLARK, September 23, 1799. Isham Clark, surety.

JAMES BROWN and ELIZABETH WOODY, May 13, 1794. James Brown, Jr., surety. Consent of William Woody, father of Elizabeth.

JAMES BROWN and RHODA REESE, October 2, 1792. John Reese, surety. Consent of Sloman Reese, father of Rhoda.

GEORGE BROWN and SARAH BROWN, November 24, 1783. Julius Jones, surety. Consent of Sarah Brown, mother of the above Sarah.

SHADRACK BROWN and HANNAH MITCHELL, October 15, 1787. Isaac Mitchell, surety. Consent of John Mitchell, father of Hannah.

SHADRACK BROWN and TABITHA HALL, October 14, 1799. Elisha Hall, surety. Consent of Magdalean Hall, mother of Tabitha.

JOHN BUFORD and RHODY SHREWSBURY, December 22, 1786. Charles Caffery, surety. Consent of Elizabeth Shrewsbury, mother of Rhody.

WILLIAM WALTON BUSH and ELIZABETH SHARP, August 22, 1796. George Sharp, surety.

STARK BROWN and TABITHA RIGBY, May 8, 1779. James Gatewood, surety.

HENRY BROWN and SUSANNA HIX, November 5, 1793. Patrick Hix, surety. Certificate of Susanna that she is of age. Witnesses, Patrick Hix and Caty Hix.

CLAYBURN BROWN and SARAH HARMON, March 8, 1781. Peter Harmon, surety.

EDWIN BARKER and ELANDER PORTER, July 16, 1796. Thomas Huddleston, surety.

ROBERT CHURCH and MATTY SHARP, August 27, 1787. Adam Sharp, surety.

DUDLEY CALLAWAY and PATTY TRENT, December 12, 1778. John Callaway, surety. Consent of Henry Trent, father of Patty.

AARON CAMPBELL and GRACEY WILLIAMSON, March 25, 1795. James Williamson, surety.

MEREDITH COMPTON and SARAH BOARD, December 11, 1795. Lewis Cundiff, surety. Consent of William Board, father of Sarah.

CHARLES CREASEY and JUDITH DOWDY, November 29, 1797. William Dowdy, surety. Certificate of Judith that she is of lawful age.

JOHN CREWS and LUCY HARDWICK, January 26, 1795. Robert Hardwick, surety.

CLAIBOURN CREASY and SUCKEY WITT, July 26, 1797. John Witt, surety.

ROYAL CHILDRESS and ELIZABETH COWARD, November 16, 1796. Reuben Cowhard, surety.

JOHN CAMPBELL and NANCY JONES, September 19, 1785. Stephen Pratt, surety. Consent of Martin Jones, father of Nancy.

DANIEL CLYBURN and ANNA FREEMAN, November 2, 1795. James Freeman, surety.

SAMUEL COBBS and ANN NOELL, August 27, 1787. Henry Jeter, surety. Consent of Corn's. Noell and Salley Noell, parents of Ann.

JESSE COBBS and ELIZABETH McCOY, July 24, 1780. Charles Cobbs, surety.

JOHN COBBS and SARAH McCOY, January 24, 1782. Jesse Cobbs, surety.

ROLLEY CROUCH and MARY ANN WITT, January 30, 1786. John Witt, surety.

CHARLES CRUMP and RHODA GRAY, November 26, 1798. William Gray, surety.

STEPHEN CALLAHAM and FEBEY McCARTEE, December 13, 1796. Martin Mason, surety. Consent of Elizabeth Callaham.

ROBERT CLARK and ELIZABETH BULLOCK, October 23, 1781. Josias Bullock, surety.

JESSE CLARK and LUCY HATCHER, February 13, 1796. Hardaway Hatcher, surety. Consent of Julius Hatcher, Sr., the father of Lucy.

JOSEPH CLARK and ELIZABETH KARN, February 25, 1793. Abraham Karn, surety.

FRANKLIN CREASEY and SIDNEY NEWMAN, December 10, 1793. Nimrod Newman, surety.

CHARLES CLAY and EDITHA DAVIES, June 27, 1796. Henry Landon Davies, surety.

JOSEPH CROUCH and SARAH WITT, January 17, 1792. John Witt, surety.

DAVID CARTER and ANNE DEREFILL, April 11, 1800. William Meador, surety. Certificate of Anne, asking that license be granted.

ADAM CARSON and PEGGY PAGAN, December 2, 1794. James Otey, surety. Certificate of Peggy that she is of age.

ADAM CARNES and MARY McCLANAHAN, March 1, 1786. Absalom McClanahan, surety. Consent of Michael Kern, father of Adam.

AUGUSTINE CARTER and NANCY PULLEN, August 2, 1792. John Carter, surety. Consent of Nancy herself.

JOHN COOPER and MACKARIA HOWELL, September 11, 1786. Samuel Burnett, surety.

11

JOHN CRAGHEAD and BETSEY ROBINSON, October 28, 1799. John Ayers, surety.
Consent of Lucy Robinson, mother of Betsey, also states that
Betsey is of age.

JAMES CLAGG and JUDITH WATSON, December 4, 1800. Johnson Watson, surety.

ISHAM CUNDIFF and POLLY OWENS, April 14, 1800. Jonathan Cundiff, surety.
Consent of Elijah Cundiff, father of Isham. Also consent of
Owen Owens and Mary Owens, parents of Polley.

BIRD CREESEY and POLLY DOWDY, October 24, 1794. William Dowdy, surety.
Consent of William Dowdy.

JAMES CALLAWAY and SUSANNAH WHITE, July 12, 1784. Lance Woodward, surety.
Consent of Stephen White, the father of Susannah.

WADDY COBBS and PEGGY GWATKINS, March 24, 1788. Samuel Cobbs, surety.

MICAJAH CLARKE and MAKEY GATEWOOD, March 14, 1786. James Gatewood,
surety. Consent of Robert Clark, father of Micajah.

ROBERT COWAN and ELIZABETH IRVINE, widow, June 8, 1769. Isham Talbot,
surety. Consent of Elizabeth.

JOHN CARTER and POLLEY PULLEN, February 26, 1789. Charles Caffery, surety.
Consent of Moses Pullen, father of Polley.

GEORGE CANNADA and CRETE DOWDY, June 27, 1796. Hundley Dowdy, surety.
Certificate of John & Hundley Dowdy that Crete is of age.

SHADRACK CUNDIFF and SALLEY FELKINS, January 12, 1799. John Felkins,
surety.

ELISHA CUNDIFF and ELIZABETH PRICE, August 26, 1789. Hatton Price, surety.
Consent of Thomas Price, father of Elizabeth, and of Mary Cundiff,
mother of Elisha.

WILLIAM CORLEY and ELIZABETH WRIGHT, June 1, 1798. James Asbury, surety.
Consent of John Wright.

WILLIAM COLDBURN and ELIZABETH BURGES, 26th _____, 1793. William
Burges, surety.

PATRICK COYLE and SUSANNAH BUNCH, April 8, 1793. William Scott, surety.
Consent of James Bunch, father of Susannah.

JIMMY CUNDIFF and LUCY BROWN, March 29, 1800. Jesse Brown, surety.
Consent of Daniel Brown.

JOHN CREWS and CLARY MERRIT, October 4, 1798. Thomas Merritt, surety.

JOHN CAMPBELL and SALLY McCAN, March 21, 1800. John McCan, surety.

WILLIAM CAMPBELL and ELIZABETH CRUMP, February 28, 1785. John Mead, surety.
Consent of Richard Crump, father of Elizabeth.

THOMAS CHILDRESS and NANCY WIGGINTON, February ___, 1794. Thomas Barton, surety. Consent of Thos. Wittinton, dated Feb. 22, 1794.

MOSES CAMPBELL and MARY DOOLEY, December 8, 1792. Moses Dooley, surety. Consent of George Dooley, father of Mary.

JOSEPH CROCKETT and LUCY SMITH, May 22, 1786. Bird Smith, surety. Consent of Anne Smith, mother of Lucy.

JOSEPH COFER and HOPE SUTTON, March 1, 1796. Nathaniel Sutton, surety. Consent of Chris. Sutton, also states that Hope is above twenty-one years of age.

THOMAS COOPER and SARAH ANTHONY, January 8, 1762. Isham Talbot, surety. Consent of Joseph Anthony.

JOEL CALLAWAY and LUCY ABSTON, December 24, 1793. Thomas Pullen, surety. Consent of Jesse Abston, father of Lucy.

PETER CLAYWELL and JEMIMA ARTHUR, August 25, 1777. Henry Eidson, surety.

JOHN CAMPBELL and MARY BROWN, April 26, 1790. Isham Galloway, surety. Consent of Manly and Janet Brown, parents of Mary.

JOHN CALLAWAY and TABITHA TATE, spinster, March 29, 1758. James Callaway, surety.

WILLIAM CHASTAIN and LYDDA WHEAT, January 3, 1792. Zadock Wheat, surety. Consent of Joseph Wheat, father of Lydda.

WILLIAM W. CLAYTON and CLARISSA _____, March 20, 1800. Robert Snoddy, surety.

ADAM CLEMENTS and ANGNESS JOHNSON, 27th_____, 1765. Joseph Anthony, surety.

LEWIS CLAYTON and ELIZABETH WRIGHT, February 12, 1796. John Wright, surety.

CHARLES CAFFERY and REBEKAH CARTER, December 10, 1786. John Carter, surety. Consent of Merry Carter, father of Rebekah.

THOMAS CREASEY and DRUSILLA DOWDY, February 28, 1792. Alex. McCollom, surety. Consent of William and Lucinda Dowdy, parents of Drusilla.

LEWIS CUNDIFF and ELIZABETH BOARD, December 10, 1787. James Cundiff, surety. Consent of William Board, father of Elizabeth.

THOMAS CAMPBELL and MARY CHURCH, September 14, 1773. William Ewing, surety. Consent of Robert Church, father of Mary.

FRANCIS CALVERT and ELIZABETH WITT, December 20, 1791. Rowland Witt, surety.

THOMAS CAMPBELL and TEMPE HURT, January 21, 1792. James Hurt, surety.

JOHN CAPE and MARY MANN, April 25, 1791. Field Mann, surety. Certificate of Mary that she is of age.

JAMES CALLAWAY, batchelor and SARAH TATE, spinster, November 24, 1756. Ben Howard, surety.

JAMES CALLAWAY and ELIZABETH EARLY, September 22, 1777. This is not a real marriage bond, but is a letter from James Callaway to the Clerk, stating that he is to be married in a few days, and that he will sign the bond the first opportunity. Says he is enclosing Majr. Early's certificate.

CHESLEY CALLAWAY and CHRISTIANA GALLOWAY, February 24, 1785. James Bramlett, surety. Consent of John Golloway, father of Christiana.

CHARLES CALLAWAY, batchelor, and JUDITH PATE, spinster, December 14, 1768. John Callaway, surety.

JOSIAH CARTER and MARY ANTHONY, June 26, 1771. Joseph Anthony, surety.

JAMES CAMPBELL and MOLLY PATTERSON, January 13, 1798. William Patterson, surety.

LARKIN CLEVELAND and FANNY WRIGHT, February ___, 1773. David Wright, surety.

SAMUEL L. CRAWFORD and CHARLOTTE AUSTIN, June 19, 1800. Robert Austin, surety. Consent of Wm. W. Austin, father of Charlotte.

JOHN CAMPBELL and JUDITH CLARK, February 5, 1786. Christopher Clark, surety. Consent of Robert Clark, Sr.

ZACHARIAH CANDLER and RACHEL THORNHILL, January 29, 1791. Reuben Thornhill, surety. Consent of Sarah Thornhill. Also consent of Zedekiah Kandler, father of Zachariah.

ISAAC CUNDIFF and MARY ECKHOLLS, October 18, 1787. Jacob Eckhols, surety.

THOMAS COTTOM and KATY HOLLIGAN, May 28, 1793. James Holligan, surety.

PLEASANT CREASEY and BETSEY NEWMAN, May 17, 1791. Arthur Newman, surety. Consent of Nimrod Newman, father of Betsey.

THOMAS L. CLAYTON and DICY WRIGHT, March 26, 1803. Francis Hunter, surety. Consent of John Wright, father of Dicy.

GEORGE CRUMP and MARY GRAY, June 23, 1791. William Gray, surety. Certificate of Mary that she is of age. Witnessed by William and Alexander Gray.

HENRY CHEEKE and JENNY HANCOCK, September 24, 1797. James Eckhols, surety. Certificate of Jenny that she is of age.

JOHN CADWALLENDAR and MARY COLLINS, July 27, 1791. Elisha Cundiff, surety. Consent of Sary Collins, mother of Mary.

14

JOHN WILLIS CLAYTON and LUCINDA DOUGLASS, March 21, 1797. Thos. L.
    Clayton, surety.

HUGH CARR, batchelor, and ELIZABETH FINLEY, spinster, September 15, 1772.
    Certificate of James and Agness Finley that Elizabeth is willing,
    etc.

WILLIAM CRUMPTON and SARAH ADAMS, December 8, 1800. William Adams,
    surety. Consent of Ann Adams, mother of Sarah.

ZACHARIAH CALLAWAY and SUSANNA MILLER, December 18, 1774. Robert
    Alexander, surety. Consent of Simon and Ann Miller, parents of
    Susanna.

JONATHAN CONSOLVER and MILLEY ROBERTSON, April 8, 1794. James Conway,
    surety. Certificate of Milley that she is of age, name spelled
    "Robinson".

WILLIAM CUNDIFF and SARAH PATTERSON, December 26, 1791. Andrew Patterson,
    surety. Consent of Joseph Patterson, father of Sarah.

SAMUEL CLEMENS and PAMELIA GOGGIN, October 23, 1797. Samuel Hancock,
    surety. Certificate of Pamelia that she is of age.

ROBERT CRAIG and KITTURAH HILTON, January 6, 1795. Jeremiah Hilton,
    surety. Consent of Lucy Hilton, mother of Kitturah.

JOHN CLAYTOR and CHARLOTTE LEFTWICH, January 9, 1792. Samuel Mitchell,
    surety. Consent of Thos. Leftwich, the father of Charlotte.

JOHN CHASTEEN and ELIZABETH CLARKE, November 7, 1785. Daniel Asbury,
    surety.

CHARLES CARTER and DINAH LAMBERT, October 7, 1787. George Lambert, surety.

ANDREW COWAN and REBECKAH PATTERSON, February 8, 1794. Andrew Black,
    surety. Consent of Jos. Patterson, father of Rebeckah.

MATTHIAS CANE and RHODY GOODMAN, June 30, 1794. John Goodman, surety.
    Consent of Bartlett Goodman, father of Rhody.

HENRY DOOLEY and SEDE WOOD, August 7, 1797. Josiah Wood and Peter Fitzhugh,
    sureties. Certificate of Sede that she is of age, etc.

JAMES DONOHO and ELIZABETH LOWRY, January 26, 1789. Simmons Everette,
    surety. Certificate of Elizabeth herself.

STEPHEN DOOLEY and MATILDA BUSH, August 26, 1778. Jacob Dooley, surety.
    Consent of Patty Bush.

JAMES DUNCAN and MARY ANN BRIGHT, February 26, 1787. Edward Gregory,
    surety.

15

ELISHA DuVAL and LUCY H. CRAINE, April 14, 1798. John Craine, surety.

NEHEMIAH DOWELL and MOLLY BOARD, October 13, 1789. Micajah Dowell, surety.
    Consent of James Board, father of Molly.

AARON DEWITT and SALLEY VAUGHAN, January 7, 1793. Walter Williams, surety.
    Consent of Lucy Wright, mother of Salley Baughan.

THOMAS DOUGHERTY and SARAH GOGGIN, June 15, 1778. Stephen Goggin, Senr.,
    surety.

CHARLES DABNEY and LUSANNY BLANKINSHIP, January 19, 1796. Stephen Pratt,
    surety. Consent of Ann Blankinship, mother of Lusanny.

HENRY DOOLEY and RACHELL McCLANAHAN, December 21, 1785. William McClanahan,
    surety. Consent of Thomas McClanhan, father of Rachell.

WILLIAM DISHMAN and SALLY SALMON, February 2,1784. John Salmon, Junr.,
    surety. Consent of John Salmon, the father of Sally.

CHARLES DONOHO and SALLY BROOKS, August 3, 1784. John McHailing, surety.
    Consent of Robi Brooks, father of Sally.

THOMAS DOOLEY and JANNY VAUGHAN, March 14, 1794. William Stone, surety.

JAMES DIXON and SUSANNA HELM, August 11, 1772. James Patterson, surety.
    Consent of Moses Helm, father of Susanna.

WILLIAM DICKERSON and FRANKEY MAYS, March 18, 179___. Jason Meador,
    surety. Consent of James Mayse.

JOHN DOOLY, batchelor, and ELIZABETH BIRKS, spinster, May 20, 1763.
    Henry Dooly, surety. Consent of John Birks.

JAMES DAVIDSON, JUNR. and JANET COCKRANE, February 6, 1779. James
    Davidson, Sr., surety. Consent of Samuel and Mary Cockran,
    parents of Janet.

DAVID DAVISON and ELIZABETH COCKRAN, August 23, 1779. James Davison,
    surety. Consent of Samuel Cockran, father of Elizabeth.

JOHN DOWNING and RACHEL DOOLING, March 23, 1778. Stephen Dooley, surety.

WILLIAM DAVENPORT and MARY NEAL, January 15, 1793. Jacob Wade, surety.
    Consent of William Wright and Ann Wright to marry "our daughter
    Mary Neal".

WILLIAM DRURY and REBECCA COLEBURN, February 12, 1793. John Coleburn,
    surety. Consent of Portlock Drury, one of the parents of
    William.

JOHN DOUGHMAN and MOLLY BARGER, March 24, 1792. John Barger, surety.

WILLIAM DURHAM and POLLY HIX, February 26, 1798. Dennis McCormack,
    surety. Consent of Philip Hix, father of Polly.

MICAJAH DOWELL and FANNY MEADOR, February 5, 1787. Jeremiah Meador, surety. Consent of Ambrous Meador, father of Fanny.

ISHAM DAVIS and ELIZABETH GILLIAM, February 4, 1796. Richard Gilliam, surety.

EDWARD DONOHO, batchelor, and RACHEL McDONALD, spinster, May 5, 1772. Isaac McDonald, surety. Certificate of Rachel that she is of age.

PETER DENT and MILLEY DOLLARD, May 5, 1789. Lamaster Cooksey, surety. Consent of Milley herself.

EZEKIEL DOWNING and RACHEL BROWN, January 30, 1778. Thomas Brown, surety. Consent of Thomas Brown.

JOHN DELLICE and SALLEY WHITE, February 11, 1795. Joseph White, surety.

JOSEPH DICKSON and ANN CARSON, March 5, 1771. Alexr. Dobbins, surety.

AMOS DAWSON and SARAH ADKINS, March 5, 1792. Thomas Palmer, surety. Consent of Rolin Adkins, father of Sarah.

WILLIAM DABNEY and BECKEY ECKHOLS, September 4, 1793. Jacob Eckhols, surety.

JACOB DOOLEY and BETTY BUSH, April 30, 1778. David Wright, surety. Consent of Martha Bush, mother of Betty.

LEWIS DEAREN and OBEDIENCE HURT, June 18, 1796. James Cundiff, surety. Consent of James Hurt, father of Obedience.

GEORGE DAWSON and MARY MITCHELL, March 28, 1796. Enos Mitchell, surety.

EPHRAIM DOOLEY and BETSEY GATSON, January 19, 1793. Benjamin Palmore, surety. Consent of Petor Gitson, father of Betsey.

AARON DOOLEY and KATY DOOLEY, August 4, 1796. Moses Campbell, surety. Consent of George Dooley, father of Aaron. Certificate of Obadiah Dooley that Katy is of age.

JOHN DIXON and MARY WILSON, November 8, 1773. James Wilson, surety. Certificate that Mary agrees and is of age.

ROBERT DAVIS and ELIZABETH TRIGG, daughter of Wm. Trigg, January 27, 1783. Alexr. Cummins, surety.

GEORGE DABNEY and BETSEY ECKHOLS, January 7, 1793. John Overstreet, surety. Consent of Jacob Eckhols and Betsey Eckhols. Witnessed by James Eckhols and Becky Eckhols.

THOMAS DEWITT and ELIZABETH BAUGHN, August 3, 1795. William Hensley, surety. Consent of James and Abigal Dewitt, parents of Thomas. Certificate of Elizabeth that she is of age.

NATHANIEL DAVIS and POLLY HENRY TATE, July 25, 1799. Nathaniel Tate, surety.

ALLEN DRAKE and JEMIMAH HIX, November 26, 1787. Phillip Hix, surety.

HENRY DAVIS and JUDAH STRATTON, September 13, 1791. William Stratton, surety. Consent of Henry Stratton, father of Judah.

RICHARD DAVIS and MARY JOHNSON, September 26, 1785. Zackry Davis, surety. Consent of William Johnson, father of Mary.

WILLIAM DENT and ESTHER BOARD, October 23, 1800. John Meador, surety. Consent of John Board.

WILLIAM DICKERSON, of Cumberland County, and ROSEANNA JORDAN, January 2, 1790. James Dunum, Jr., surety. Consent of Absolem Jordan, father of Roseanna.

CHARLES DABNEY and BETSEY HALE, March 26, 1798. Henry Davis, surety. Consent of John Hale, father of Betsey.

RICHARD DOGGETT, batchelor, and RHODA EVANS, widow, February 23, 1761. Ish. Talbot, surety.

WILLIAM DAVIDSON and NANCY SCOTT, October 19, 1792. Cosby Scott, surety. Consent of John Scott, father of Nancy; also says she is of age.

SAMUEL DAVISON and EUNICE CREASEY, December 24, 1791. Benjamin Davison, surety. Consent of Thomas Creasey, father of Eunice.

CLABOURN DOWDY and AGNESS WITT, August 22, 1795. John Wigginton and Joseph Thurman, sureties. Certificate of Agness that she is twenty-one years of age.

JOHN DOOLEY and _____ FORSYTHE, March 5, 1783. Thomas Dooley, Senr., surety. Consent for marriage with John Dooley saying she is of full age, but certificate is not signed.

WILLIAM DOWDY and ELIZABETH CREASEY, January 27, 1795. Chas. Creasey, surety. Consent of John Creasey, father of Elizabeth.

JEREMIAH DISHMAN and NANCY MILLER, November 6, 1782. Simon Miller, Jr., surety.

MICAJAH DOSS and MARY SWAIN, December 19, 1792. Charles Swain, surety.

JOHN DOWDY, JR. and MARY FOSTER, April 4, 1792. Ezekiel Dowdy, surety. Consent of John Foster, father of Mary.

RICHARD DURRETT and ESTHER SMITH, December 12, 1793. William Leftwich, surety. Certificate of Esther Smith that she is of age.

JOEL DAVENPORT and SUSANNA WILLIAMSON, June 14, 1790. Moses Chambers, surety. Consent of John Williamson, father of Susanna.

WILLIAM DALE and JEMIMA JACKSON, October 26, 1778. Jarvis Jackson, surety.

THOMAS DOBYNS and NANCY McGLOTHLAN, December 25, 1797. John McGlothlan, surety. Consent of John McGlothlan. Witnessed by William McGlothlan.

18

ROBERT DELLIS and PHEBE MORGAN, September 22, 1800. Reese Morgan, surety. Consent of Thos. and Susanna Morgan, parents of Phebe.

THOMAS DAY and ELIZABETH MOODY, July 25, 1785. Joseph Wright, surety. Consent of Thomas Moody, father of Elizabeth.

EZEKIEL DOWDY and JANE FREEMAN, August 9, 1787. James Freeman, surety.

JOEL DAVENPORT and MARGET RAMSEY, February 25, 1796. William Davenport, surety.

ROBERT DUDLEY DAWSON of Amherst County, and MARY LIGHTFOOT SLAUGHTER, of Bedford, October 31, 1782. Reuben Slaughter, surety.

STEPHEN DOOLY and MOLLY BRAMBLETT, July 24, 1781. John Downing, surety.

ROBERT RUSSELL DIXON and MARY McCLARD, February 6, 1789. John Howell, surety. Certificate of Mary that she is of age.

JOHN DOOLEY and MOLLEY SAMMONS, November 10, 1783. Stephen Dooley, surety. Consent of John Sammons, father of Molley.

WILLIAM DOLLARD and NANCY CARNER, November 22, 1800. John Carner, surety.

WILLIAM DOUGLASS and KITTY GISSAG SLAUGHTER, January 26, 1795. Reuben Slaughter, surety.

OBADIAH DOOLEY and ANN ERWIN, March 22, 1796. Jonas Erwin, surety.

ROBERT DELBRIDGE and MILLEY GUTHRY, November 26, 1798. John Guthry, surety.

NATHAN DABNEY and JENNY YOUNGER, December 21, 1789. Jesse Grub, surety. Consent of Ann Younger.

HENRY DEARDORF and MARGARETT WATSON, March 20, 1798. James Watson, surety.

JOHN DIXON and MARTHA ARTHUR, December 4, 1795. Thomas Arthur, surety. Consent of William Arthur, the father of Martha.

JOSHUA DALLAS and NANCY KEETH, December 15, 1788. John Overstreet, surety. Consent of Elizabeth Keeth, mother of Nancy.

JAMES DALTON and POLLY ADAMS, April 23, 1798. Thomas Adams, surety. Certificate of Polly that she is of age.

MOSES DOOLEY and HULDA SHARP, April 2, 1796. John Sharp, surety.

GEORGE DOOLEY and AMILY CALLAWAY, December 10, 1792. Daniel Neal, surety. This certificate filed with bond: "This is to cartify that Susanna Hilton the mother of Amealy Callaway and James Hilton, the farthar in Law is willin that Gorge Duly shall take out lisons to marry hir." Signed "Amealy Callaway".

HUNDLEY DOWDY and ELENOR CREASEY, December 5, 1796. John Creasey, surety.

JOHN DOBBINS and THEODOTIA KING, June 7, 1800. John Gibbs, surety.
Consent of William King, father of Theodotia.

THOMAS DELANY and MARTHA FERRALL, December 22, 1774. Chris. Lynch, surety.
Consent of William Farrell, father of Martha.

JEREMIAH EARLY and MARY STITH, December 23, 1773. William Mead, surety.

JOSHUA EARLY, batchelor, and MARY LEFTWICH, spinster, April 26, 1763.
I. Talbot, surety. Consent of Augt. Leftwich, father of Mary.

ABNER EARLY and DOSHEY ANDERSON, February 12, 1791. Charles Price, surety.
Consent of Jacob Anderson, father of Doshey.

JOHN EDGAR and REBECKAH HOOLE, April 18, 1796. David Hoole, surety.
Consent of Charles Hoole, father of Rebeckah.

CHARLES EADES and SARAH PIBORN, May 2, 1786. James Bramblett, surety.
Consent of Jacob Piborn, father of Sarah. Certificate that
Sarah is of age.

JAMES EARLY and SOPHIA GATEWOOD, March 24, 1785. James Gatewood, surety.
Consent of Joshua Early.

GEORGE L. ENGLISH and ANN SMITH, August 14, 1790. Richard Thurman,
surety. Consent of John Smith, father of Ann.

HENRY EIDSON and NANCY BUNCH, December 16, 1797. Benjamin White, surety.
Consent of James and Polly Bunch, parents of Nancy.

BENJAMIN ELLIS and TELLITHA MITCHELL, January 16, 1792. John Mitchell,
surety. Consent of Tellitha Mitchell.

SPENCER ELLIS and DICEY PRATT, September 6, 1796. Archibald Frith, surety.
Consent of Dicey, stating that she has no guardian, etc.

JAMES ENGLISH and ANN ROBINSON, March 17, 1794. Arthur Robinson, surety.
Consent of Lucy Robinson, mother of Ann.

JACOB EARLY and ELIZABETH ROBERSON, March 18, 1767. John Roberson, surety.
Consent of Elizabeth.

WILLIAM EARLY and PELETIAH JONES WALKER, October 7, 1793. James Quarles,
surety. Certificate of Palatiah Jones Walker that she is of
age, etc.

JACOB ECKOLS and MARY CAGEL, July 7, 1761. Peter Nerdeman, surety.

NATHAN EAKIN and SUSANNA PRESTON, June 2, 1785. Stephen Preston, surety.
Memo. The fathers consent given in person.

WILLIAM EDGAR and PAMELLA EWING, June 22, 1789. John Ewing, surety.

JOHN EUBANK and SARAH PALMORE, December 25, 1797. Jesse Lockett, surety. Consent of Benjamin Palmore, father of Sarah.

CHATHAM EWING and ELIZABETH CAMPBELL, April 14, 1790. James Campbell, surety.

WILLIAM EALY and MARY RALLINGS, October 23, 1780. William Thomas, surety. Consent of Mary Rolings, mother of Mary.

MARK EVANS and TEMPY BRATCHER, February 24, 1800. John Bratcher, surety.

MITCHELL EWING and PHEBE COX, December 27, 1797. Matthew McMullen. Consent of Wm. Ewing, states Phebe is of age.

JACOB ECKHOLS and JENNY JONES, July 12, 1796. Charles Caffery, surety. Consent of Julius Jones, father of Jenny.

EDWARD EIDSON and ELIZABETH EIDSON, March 12, 1800. William Eidson, surety. Consent of Boyce Eidson, father of Elizabeth.

WILLIAM EIDSON and SALLEY HARRIS, May 15, 1800. Henry Eidson, surety. Consent of Nathaniel Harris, father of Sally.

JOSEPH EADS and ELIZABETH HUDDLESTON, December 19, 1796. Henry Huddleston, surety. Consent of Mary Huddleston, the mother of Elizabeth.

WILLIAM EMBREY and FRANCES MILAM, January 18, 1786. James Spence, surety. Consent of Anne Milam, mother of Frances.

ACHILLES EUBANK and MARY BUSH, July 19, 1779. Jacob Dooley, surety. Consent of Martha Bush.

URIAH ELLIS and USSANNAH MOORMAN, March 26, 1794. William Ellis, surety. Certificate of Susannah that she is of age.

JOHN ELLIS and NANCY WILLIAMS, January 2, 1794. Robert Boyle, surety. Consent of William Williams, father of Nancy.

JAMES EDGAR and PHEBE WRIGHT, April 16, 1778. Harry Innis, surety. Certificate of Phebe that she is 22 yrs. old.

JOHN ELLIOTT and ELIZABETH HOWARD, January 8, 1800. William Lowry, surety.

JAMES ECKHOLS and JENNY HANCOCK, April 6, 1791. William Dickerson, surety. Consent of Jane Hancock.

WILLIAM FERGUSON and ELIZABETH BROWN, March 7, 1787. Jeremiah Ferguson, surety. Consent of Wm. Brown, father of Elizabeth.

PLEASANT FERGUSON and NANCY PHELPS, October 6, 1785. John Ferguson, surety. Consent of John Phelps, father of Nancy.

SAMUEL FLEMING and ELIZABETH RUTHERFORD, August 5, 1774. John Forbes, surety. Consent of William Rutherford, the father of Elizabeth.

WILLIAM FRAZIER and SUSANNA GRIMES, December 20, 1785. James Flanagan, surety. Consent of Joseph and Mary Grimes, parents of Susanna.

JAMES FOWLER and SARAH DAWSON, January 26, 1786. Joseph Wilkinson, surety. Consent of John Dawson, father of Sarah.

JOHN FISHER and ELIZABETH STOTT, July 24, 1786. Simmons Everett and I. Fuqua, sureties. Consent of Isham Fuqua, which states that Elizabeth is an orphan and is now bound to him.

THOMAS FRITH and RUTH A. GOFF, February 24, 1800. John Goff, surety. Consent of Joseph Goff, father of Ruth.

JESSE FEARS and NANCY ESTES, April 23, 1792. Joel Preston, surety. Consent of Benjamin Estes.

WILLIAM FRITH and RHODA MASON, August 27, 1796. Joel Compton, surety. Consent of Elizabeth (Keenan), mother of Rhoda Mason.

AARON FUQUA and ELIZABETH CARTER, January 25, 1796. Moses Pullen, surety. Consent of Merry Carter, father of Elizabeth.

ROBERT FITZHUGH and ANNE EDGAR, June 28, 1783. Joseph Parish, surety. Consent of John Edgar, father of Anne.

JAMES FOSTER, JR. and ELIZABETH WIGGONTON, October 16, 1792. Thornton O'Neal, surety. Consent of Jhon Wiggonton that the parents are willing.

JOHN FARTHING and MARY MARTIN, November 26, 1779. James Martin, surety. Consent of Robert and Sarah Martin, parents of Mary.

ABRAHAM FLEMING and FANNY MARTIN, November 26, 1772. John Forbes, surety. Certificate of Samuel Hairston that Fanny is of age and has lived separate from her parents for several years.

WILLIAM FISHER and MARY SCOTT, April 6, 1793. Cozbi Scott, surety. Consent of John Scott, father of Mary; also states that she is of age.

EDMUND FRANKLIN and ROSENAH NUMAN, December 22, 1788. Thomas Creesy, surety. Consent of some Numan (cannot read the first name).

OBEDIAH FULKS and MARTHA BLANKENSHIP, October 15, 1787. Richard Wilbourn, surety. Consent of Joseph Blankenship, the father of Martha.

WILLIAM FOWLER and JINNEY OGLESBY, December 11, 1799. Jacob Oglesby, surety. Consent of David Oglesby, father of Jinney.

CALEB FUQUA and MILLE ABSTON, November 24, 1800. Moses Fuqua, surety.

SAMUEL FIDLER and ELIZABETH MORLAN, September 22, 1794. William Morlan, surety.

JOSEPH FEAZEL and RACHEL SINKLER, November 24, 1800. Robert Sinkler, Jr., surety.

WILLIAM FREEMAN and SALLY PARKER, October 26, 1798. David Parker, surety. Consent of John Parker, father of Sally; also consent of James Freeman, the father of William.

JOHN FOULDEN and MARY WOMACK, December 31, 1789. Thomas Carver, surety. Consent of Sarah Womack, mother of Mary. Witnesses, William and Rhoda Womack.

WILLIAM FERRELL and PRUDENCE HALLEY, January 29, 1787. William Halley, surety. Consent of Francis Halley, father of Prudence.

ADAM FOULDEN and SALLEY TAYLOR, February 26, 1794. William Bradley, surety. Consent of William and Mary Taylor, parents of Salley.

THOMAS FARMER, widower, and JANE BABER, spinster, March 19, 1770. William Baber, surety. Consent of Robt. Baber, the father of Jane.

JACOB FREDERICK and CATHRINE KINZER, November 6, 1792. John Kinzer, surety. The following note from Wm. Ewing to the Clerk, is filed: "Capt. Rice, Sir: Mr. Jacob Frederick & Miss Catherine Kinzer our new neighbours children are about to wed — I am well informed all parties are willing for it so to be — I tell them they cannot do without your aid."

DRURESTER FOSTER and MARY PRATT, April 4, 1786. Abner Foster, surety. Consent of James and Mary Foster, parents of Drurester; also of Mary Pratt, mother of Mary.

WILLIAM FRENCH and ELANOR MURPHEY, June 10, 1779. Robert Field, surety. Consent of Ellender herself.

WILLIAM FITZSIMMONS and LUCY GARDNER HUGHES, October 26, 1795. Benj. Hatcher, surety. Consent of Rice Hughes, the grandfather of Lucy. Her parents dead.

JOHN BRYANT FRANKLIN and MARGET NUMAN, April 23, 1792. Edmund Franklin, surety. Consent of some Numan (cannot read the first name).

JAMES FARMER and BETSY HUBBARD, January 17, 1780. James Adams, surety. Consent of Sam'l Hubbard, the father of Betsy.

JAMES FOLDEN and ELIZABETH TALER, February 23, 1791. Thomas Bradley, surety. Consent of John Taler, father of Elizabeth.

JAMES FLOURNOY and PEGGY CUNDIFF, February 28, 1785. John Hancock, surety. Consent of James Flournoy, the father of James. Witness, Jacob Flournoy. Also consent of Mary Cundiff, mother of Peggy.

SAMUEL FIELDS and MILLE HURT, April 28, 1800. James Hurt, surety.

WILLIAM FINNEY and ELIZABETH DEWITT, October 11, 1785. William Williams, surety. Consent of _____ Dewitt, parent of Elizabeth. (Cannot tell whether the first name is Henry or Mary.)

PETER FITZHUGH and NANCY DAWSON, June 27, 1785. Robert Fitzhugh, surety. Consent of John Dawson, father of Nancy.

JOHN FOURQUERAN and MARY GUTHRY, February 26, 1772. George Callaway, surety. Consent of the parent of Mary, but cannot make out name.

ARCHER FRANKLIN and MARY WEEKES, December 24, 1800. Elijah Weekes, surety. Consent of George Weekes, father of Mary.

EDMUND FRANKLIN and BETSEY PRYOR, March 15, 1794. William Pryor, surety. Consent of Hanes (or Haris) Pryor, father of Betsey.

THOMAS FRANKLIN and MARGARET CAMPBELL, July 6, 1779. Lewis Franklin, surety. Consent of James Campbell, father of Margaret.

JAMES FREEMAN and NANCY DOWDY, November 18, 1796. John Dowdy, surety.

SAMUEL FIDLER and FRANCES MAJOR, December 25, 1797. Bernard Feezel, surety.

WILLIAM FARMER and MARY DRURY, January 23, 1792. Joseph Thurman, surety.

JOHN ARMOUR FINLEY and ELIZABETH COOK, May 14, 1785. Samuel Finley, surety.

MOSES FUQUA and DELPHA HOWARD, December 23, 1800. Joel Estes, surety.

WILLIAM FUQUA and SARAH PRATHER, February 12, 1769. Thomas Prather, surety.

JOHN FITZPATRICK and BEHETHALINE BRENT, October ___, 1762. John Talbot, surety.

JOHN FRANKLIN and NANCY BOOTHE, November 14, 1796. William Boothe, surety.

JOHN GILL and PEGGY PITTMAN, October 13, 1778. Robert Alexander, surety. Certificate that Peggy is of age.

JOHN GRAY and REBECKAH CAMPBELL, May 31, 1796. Wm. Halley and Michael Rupert, sureties. Consent of Thos. Campbell, father of Rebeckah.

JOSHUA GOAD and SALLY TOLER, December 9, 1799. Stephen Toler, surety.

EDMUND GOODE and SALLEY BRANCH, November 19, 1791. James Branch, surety. Consent of Susannah Branch, mother of Salley.

ALEXANDER GIBBS and HANNAH GILBERT, April 3, 1777. Samuel Gilbert, surety.
Certificate of Hannah that she is more than twenty-one.

JAMES GILBERT and MARTHA GASH, Nov. 7, 1786. Thos. McGlothlin, surety.
Certificate of Martha that she is of age.

THOS. GILBREATH and ELIZABETH HAYS, May 30, 1779. John Hays, surety.

ANDREW GRUBB and PATSEY THORP, September 11, 1800. Nathan Thorp, surety.
Consent of Solomon Thorp, father of Patsey.

BENJAMIN GALLOWAY and RHODA ROBERTS, August 23, 1783. Richard Roberts,
surety. Consent of Christan Roberts, mother of Rhoda.

DAVID GREEN and ANN JONES, December 27, 1785. Charles Harman, surety.

DAVID GIBBS and JEMIMA JONES, August 13, 1778. Robert Stevens, surety.
Consent of William Jones.

JARRETT GILLIAM and ANN GILLIAM, March 24, 1787. Richard Gilliam, Jr.,
surety. Consent of Richard Gilliam, father of Ann.

FRANCIS GADDY and JUDITH BOCOCK, August 28, 1795. George Gaddy, surety.
Consent of Elijah Bocock, father of Judith.

ARCHELAUS GILLIAM and NANCY BOSWELL, March 28, 1796. John Boswell, Jr.,
surety.

BARTHOLOMEW GADDY and MARTHA CREWS, October 18, 1791. John Taylor, surety.
Certificate of Martha that she is of age.

BARTHOLOMEW ADAMS GASKINS and RACHEL WOOD DONOTHAN, May 7, 1793. Rhuben
Dollard, surety.

JOHN GOFF, JR. and FANNY TENNISON, February 13, 1796. Samuel Stanley,
surety.

ROBERT GOODMAN and ANN NEAL, February 24, 1796. John Goodman, surety.
Consent of Zephannah Neal, parent of Ann.

DAVID GOODMAN and NANCY DEAL, February 11, 1789. Thomas Phillips, surety.
Consent of Sarah Parker, mother of Nancy Deal.

ELIJAH GATES and ELIZABETH CHILES, February 23, 1782. James Steptoe, surety.
Consent of John Chiles, father of Elizabeth.

JOHN GRANT and EDY BROWN, July 19, 1794. No surety.

WILLIAM GARRETT and MOLLY MAYBERRY, December 1, 1800. Henry Mayberry,
surety. Consent of Frederick Mayberry, father of Mary.

JAMES GRAYSON and BATHSHEBA PHELPS, May 21, 1791. John Phelps, surety.

WILLIAM GIBBS and WILMUTH NANCE, November 24, 1794. Paschal Nance, surety.

WILLIAM GATSON and ELIZABETH DOOLEY, January 19, 1793. Benj. Palmore, surety. Consent of Rebeckah Dooley, the mother of Elizabeth.

JOSEPH GOING and JUDITH POLLARD, September 20, 1780. John Mitchell, surety.

THOS. GASH and ELIZABETH GILBERT, July 18, 1763. Peter Brooks, surety. Consent of Michael Gash and Elizabeth Gash.

PRESTON GILBERT and JEMIMAH COCK, December 30, 1769. Michael Gash, surety. Consent of George Cock, father of Jemimah.

ABRAM GOFF and SALLY RUFF, July 25, 1798. John Mann and Richard Moss, sureties.

JOHN GOFF and SEBIA HALLEY, May 19, 1800. Sanford Halley, surety. Consent of Francis Halley, father of Sebia.

WILLIAM GOAD and NANCY GOAD, January 14, 1797. Thomas Goad, surety. Consent of Robert Goad, father of Nancy.

BENJAMIN GILBERT and HANNAH BUTLER, August 4, 1779. Benjamin Terrill, surety. Consent of Edward Butler, father of Hannah.

MICHAEL GILBERT and SALLY MOOREMAN, February 2, 1779. Jacob Moon, Jr., surety.

MICHAEL GASH, JR. and MOLLY BATES, July 10, 1778. Robert Stevens, surety. Consent of William Bates, father of Molly.

WILLIAM GLASS and SARAH PURSLEY, February 1, 1775. William Pursley, surety.

WILLIAM GARDE (or GERDE) and PATSY PARSONS, December 20, 1792. Jas. Martindale, surety.

STEPHEN GOGGIN and RACHEL MOORMAN, December 21, 1773. Stephen Goggin, Senr., surety. Consent of Rachel herself.

BARTHOLOMEW GADDY and ELIZABETH THORP, June 29, 1784. George Gaddy, surety. Consent of Elizabeth herself.

JACOB GRUBBS and NANCY TURNER, September 26, 1800. James Turner, surety.

MARTIN GREER and MARY WRIGHT, February 25, 1788. Joseph Wright, surety.

JAMES GREER and ANNE LOW, widow, April 28, 1767. Parmenas Haynes, surety.

DANIEL GALLOWAY and REBECKAH WOODWARD, September 8, 1787. Ric'd Woodward, surety. Consent of William Woodward.

CHARLES GWATKINS and MARY CALLAWAY, November 6, 1767. Richard Calloway, surety.

ARCHIBALD GALLOWAY and MOLLY FOLDEN, December 26, 1796. John Folden, surety.

HENRY GREER and SUSANNA HATCHER, September 24, 1792. Samuel Hatcher, surety. Consent of Ben Hatcher.

ALEXANDER GRAY and MARY W. CRUMP, December 24, 1791. Chas. Crump, surety. Consent of Susannah Crump, mother of Mary W. Crump.

BAILEY GREENWOOD and NANCY JARVIS, April 22, 1779. John Jarvis, surety.

JOHN GOGGIN and LUCY BRANCH, September 8, 1777. Stephen Goggin, surety. Consent of Olive Branch, father of Lucy.

JOHN GUTHRY and NANCY CRUMP, November 29, 1786. Robert Baker, surety. Consent of Richard and Elizabeth Crump, the parents of Nancy.

JOSEPH GIBSON and JUDA GIBSON, date unreadable. John Quarles, surety. Consent of John Gibson, father of Juda, which is dated in year 1762.

STEPHEN GOGGIN and SUSANNA TERRY, September 25, 1772. Robert Donald, surety.

JARRATT GILLIAM and THEODOSIA DAVIS, February 18, 1796. James Davis, surety. Consent of Elizabeth Davis of Amherst County, the mother of Theodosia.

SAMUEL GWYNN and NANCY MAGERS, May 29, 1799. Jesse Hix, surety. Certificate of Nancy herself, asking that license be issued.

JACK (JOHN) GIBSON and HANNAH EIDSON, May 2, 1800. William Eidson, surety. Consent of Boyce Eidson, father of Hannah.

ISHAM GOING and ANNE BURNES, February 14, 1785. Benjamin Rice, surety.

RICHARD GROSS and REBEKAH SMELSER, September 4, 1786. Paulser Smelser, surety. Consent of Cathrine Smelser, mother of Rebekah.

JOHN GILL and PEGGY PITTMAN, October 13, 1778. Robert Alexander, surety.

JOHN GOWER and ELIZABETH GOWING, December 22, 1795. Isham Gowing, surety. Consent of William Gowing, father of Betsey.

SAMUEL HARDY and KEZIAH LAZENBY, November 10, 1797. Joshua Lazenby, surety. Consent of Robert Lazenby, the father of Keziah.

STEPHEN HUBARD and MARTHA H. BUFORD, January 12, 1796. Thos. Stewart, surety. Certificate from Martha H. Buford, asking that license be issued.

JOSEPH HEADEN and SARAH FARLEY BOOTH, August 23, 1797. Richard Booth and Benj. Daniel, sureties.

JOHN HENDERSON and ELIZABETH MANN, November 2, 1780. David Caldwell, surety.

PETER HUDSON and LUCY NICHOLS, November 1st, 1792. David Hudson, surety.
Consent of Lucy herself, stating she is of age.

ANDREW HODGES and BETSY BUNCH, January 28, 1784. Charles Bunch, surety.

THOMAS SMITH HUDNALL and RHODA CHAFFIN, October 6, 1794. Jeremiah
Hilton, surety. Consent of Josiah Chafen, father of Rhoda.

ROBERT HUGHES and ANNE HEARD, September 6, 1762. Alexr. Borland, surety.
Consent of Stephen Goggin "Guardian and master of Ann Heard".

ISAAC HEWITT and ELIZABETH BURTON, July 25, 1799. Isaac Sinclair, surety.
Consent of Jacob Burton, father of Elizabeth.

STEPHEN HEWITT and NANCY GIBBS, October 10, 1797. Alexr. Gibbs, surety.

CALEB HALL and ELIZABETH MASTIN, May 11th, 1776. John Forqueran, surety.

GEORGE HEARD and ANN DEAN, December 17, 1782. John Mead, surety.
Consent of Charles Dean.

THOMAS HUDDLESTON and SALLY CANNADY, January 26, 1790. John Huddleston,
surety. Consent of William Cannady, father of Sally.

SAMUEL HIBBS and EVE JAMES, October 7, 1791. John James, surety. Consent
of Eve's mother, but cannot make out the name. (perhaps Jonoby).

ANDREW HARDIE and MARTHA DOOLEY, November 7, 1781. William Moon, surety.
Consent of Rebeckah Dooley.

BENJAMIN HALL and PRICILLA STUART, February 10, 1797. Thomas Wiatt,
surety. Certificate from Alex Stuart that Priscilla is 21
years of age.

THOMAS HAMILTON and ELIZABETH WRIGHT, May 21, 1783. Stephen Dooley,
surety.

DANIEL HUDDLESTON and AGGIE HOLLIDAY, January 22, 1788. Joseph Hibbs,
surety. Consent of David Holliday, father of Aggie.

FARTHING HIX and RHODA TURNER, March 20, 1784. John Hix, surety.
Consent of Isaiah Turner, father of Rhoda.

JAMES HACKWORTH and MARY CONNER, March 5, 1788. John Williamson, surety.
Consent of George Hackworth, father of James, also consent of
John Conner, father of Mary.

JOHN HUNTER and SUSANNA PRESTON, April 16, 1785. Joel Preston, surety.
Consent of Thos. Preston.

DREWRY HARDAWAY and ANN STITH, March 23, 1779. Joseph Stith, surety.

JOSEPH HOLT and SUSANNAH SAUNDERS, October 18, 1784. Benjamin Rice, surety. Consent of Elizabeth Saunders, the mother of Susannah.

HAMPTON HAYNES and MILDRED FERRILL, March 6, 1793. Abner Ferrill, surety. Consent of Gabrel Farel, father of Mildred.

ROBERT HAWKINS and NANCY FORQUERAN, December 30, 1794. John Forqueran, surety.

ROWLAND HORSLEY and NANCY TALBOT, August 26, 1779. James Talbot, surety. Consent of Elizabeth Talbot, mother of Nancy.

LEONARD HALL and SALLEY ALLEN, December 27, 1797. Thomas Gray, surety.

BARNES HOLLOWAY and SARAH MEADOW, August 14, 1780. William Hix, surety. Consent of John Meadow, father of Sarah.

NEHEMIAH HUNDLEY and POLLEY PARKER, October 2, 1799. William Freeman, surety. Consent of John Parker.

HENRY HAYNES and TABITHA TURNER, May 17, 1784. Elijah Turner, surety.

JESSE HIX and JANE FERRILL, October 22, 1787. Dan Stockton, surety.

EDWARD HANCOCK and SARAH WOMACK, September 4, 1792. John Folden, surety. Consent signed by Edw. Hancock, Sarah Womack, Salley Daniel Womack, Anna Womack.

JOSEPH HOPPER and MARY WRIGHT, December 8, 1795. Anthony Wright, surety. Consent of John Wright.

LEVI HARRIS and TABBY HACKWORTH, November 27, 1797. William Hackworth, surety. Consent of Jos. (or Jas.) Hackworth.

WILLIAM HAYNES and AGNESS PATE, December 5, 1797. John Pate, surety. Consent of Matthew Pate, father of Agness.

JOHN NEWBY HUDSON and NANCY GOLDEN, January 27, 1797. Simon Hudson, surety. Consent of Stephen and Mary Hunt for Nancy's marriage, but does not show relationship.

JOHN HENSLEY and MARY WADE, December 24, 1792. Samuel Hensley, surety. Consent of David and Frances Wade.

EDWARD HATCHER and SARAH BORLING, November 22, 1779. David Irvine, surety.

WILLIAM HALLEY and REBECKAH FERRILL, December 12, 1785. John Otey, surety. Consent of Rebeckah herself.

JOHN HOOK and BETTY SMITH, February 29, 1772. James Donald, surety. Consent of John Smith, father of Betty.

ELIJAH HURT and POLLY OVERSTREET, December 20, 1797. Thomas Overstreet, Jr., surety. Consent of Thomas Overstreet, father of Polly.

JESSEE HALL and ELIZABETH WILLIAMS, February 27, 1797. John Thrasher, surety.

BENJAMIN HENNY and MILLY ALLEN, January 27, 1794. Stephen Hook, surety. Consent of Milly herself.

WILLIAM HARDEN and CATY WILLIAMS, September 6, 1800. James McCarty, surety. Consent of Thomas Williams, father of Caty.

DRURY HOLLAND and SALLY TURNER, December 26, 1785. Elijah Turner, surety. Consent of Elijah Turner, father of Sally.

JOHN HANCOCK and MARTHA PAYNE, February 26, 1794. Archibald Nichols, surety.

THOMAS HACKWORTH and ELIZABETH JOHNSON, January 27, 1786. Wm. Hackworth, surety. Thos. Leftwich certifies that Elizabeth is of full age.

WILLIAM HENDERSON and LOCKY TRIGG, November 22, 1779. Robt. Alexander, surety. Consent of Mary Trigg, mother of Locky.

WILLIAM HUDNALL, JR. and ELIZABETH HOGAN, October 8, 1796. William Johnson and Thomas Hudnall, sureties. Consent of Daukes Johnson, mother of Elizabeth.

JEREMIAH HATCHER and BETSY RUCKER, December 24, 1800. George Rucker, surety.

GEORGE HARDWICK and SUSANNA RICE, December 26, 1785. John Wheat, surety. Consent of Charles Rice, Sr., the father of Susanna.

OBEDIAH HOGAN and MARGET MITCHELL, September 16, 1793. Enos Mitchell, surety.

PETER HUNTER and LUCY GOFF, August 14, 1797. John Goff, surety. Consent of Joseph Goff.

BENJAMIN HENNY and EASTER AYERS, July 11, 1796. Samuel Ayres, surety. Consent of James Ayers, Sr., father of Easter.

ELISHA HALL and SARAH BEST, November 24, 1800. Levi Best, surety. Consent of Drusala Best, mother of Sarah.

JOHN HUCKEBY and FRANKEY BRANNON, January 21, 1799. Lawrence James, surety. Consent of Laurence Brannon, the father of Frankey.

JACOB HANKLE and ELIZABETH FIRSEE, January 23, 1799. Frederick Goolery, surety. Consent of Elizabeth Firsee, the mother of Elizabeth.

FRANCIS HUNTER and JANE WRIGHT, November 30, 1787. John Wright, surety.

JAMES HOBBS and MARY DOLLARD, April 22, 1799. David Lockett, surety. Consent of Reuben Dollard, father of Mary.

JAMES HILTON and SUSANNA CALLAWAY, February 14, 1789. Isaac Wade, surety. Consent of Susanna herself.

WARD HATCHER and TEMPEY GREER, August 4, 1791. John Ballard, surety. Consent of Nancy Demoss, mother of Tempey.

LEWIS HOLLIDAY and RUTH SINKLER, November 26, 1798. Charles Simmons, surety.

THOMAS HAILE and JENNY MOODEY, February 10, 1793. Samuel Moody, surety. Consent of John and Susannah Moody, the parents of Jenny.

GEORGE HANNAH and BETSEY BRATCHER, November 2, 1792. John Bratcher, surety. Consent of John Bratcher, the father of Betsey.

HENRY HUDDLESTON and PATTY LOYD, May ___, 1798. Henry Loyd, surety.

JAMES HENSLEY and SALLEY HATCHER, December 5, 1796. Jeremiah Hatcher, surety. Consent of Henry and Ann Hatcher, parents of Salley.

FRANCIS G. HARWOOD and TIRZAH BOND, June 9, 1798. Wright Bond, surety.

HENRY HURT and RHODA WRIGHT, December 24, 1798. John Wright, surety.

THOMAS HUDDLESTON and RACHEL HUDDLESTON, January 20, 1787. Benjamin Watts, surety. Consent of Dannel Huddleston, father of Rachel.

SAMUEL HUDDLESTON and SARAH WATTS, January 26, 1784. Wagman Sinclair, surety.

DAVID HOLLADAY and MARTHA SIMMONS, June 26, 1797. George Simmons, surety.

WILLIAM HAILE and SUCKEY MAXEY, October 24, 1796. William Arthur, surety.

ABRAHAM HUDDLESTON and MARY ALLEN, March 2, 1793. Daniel Huddleston, surety. Request from Ann Allen that license be issued.

SAMUEL HUFF and SARAH HIX, March 3, 1773. Peter Huff, surety. Consent of John Hix, father of Sarah.

RANDOLPH HUMPHREYS and HANNAH HAYNES, April 26, 1790. Drury Wilkerson, surety. Request from Hannah that she is of full age and that license be issued.

JOSHUA HALLEY and ELIZABETH DOUGLASS, March 12, 1792. William Halley, surety. Request from Elizabeth that license be issued, that she is of age.

GEORGE HUDDLESTON and SUSANNA SLACK, November 19, 1800. John Slack, surety. Consent of Abram Slack, the father of Susanna.

GILES HALLEY and SARAH HALLEY, January 27, 1794. Benjamin Halley, surety. Consent of John Halley, the father of Sarah.

ROBERT HARPER and MARGORY PAYNE, December 21, 1787. William Payne, surety. Consent of John Payne, father of Margory.

JOHN HUMPHREYS and MARGARET MURPHY, November 22, 1784. William Woody, surety.

SAMUEL HANCOCK and NANCY MOON, February 9, 1784. Arch'd Moon, surety.

REUBIN HUGHES and ELIZABETH ESTES, February 19, 1800. Joel Estes, surety.
Consent of Benj. Estes, father of Elizabeth.

BLACKMORE HUGHES and NANCY ROUNTREE, December 22, 1783. Samuel Roundtree,
surety. Consent of Dudley and Susannah Roundtree, parents of
Nancy.

JOHN HANCOCK and MILLEY BRAMBLETT, September 1, 1787. James Bramblett,
surety. Consent of Anay Bramblett, mother (?) of Milley.

JOHN HUDNALL and PATSEY NEWMAN, November 30, 1793. Nimrod Newman, surety.
Consent of Nimrod Newman, father of Patsey.

WILLIAM HENNY and SARAH PRESTON, December 27, 1788. Stephen Arthur, surety.
Consent signed by Mikel Henny and Mary Doss.

COLBY HURT and SENAH WRAY, October 2, 1797. James Hurt, surety. Consent
of Luke Wray, father of Senah.

JOHN HAYS and JENNY THOMPSON, August 2, 1779. Thomas Thompson, surety.
Consent of Adam Thompson, father of Jenny.

JOHN HARDWICK, JR. and JOANNA HALL, January 1, 1784. John Forqueran,
surety. Consent of Leonard Hall, father of Joanna.

WILLIAM HACKWORTH and SUSANNA ARTHUR, December 25, 1799. Levi Harris,
surety. Consent of William Arthur, father of Susanna.

JOHN HALLEY and ANNE GADDY, May 11, 1785. George Gaddy, surety. Consent
of Anna Gaddy, mother of Anne.

ABSALOM HALL and SALLEY SCOTT, September 11, 1798. William Scott, surety.

JOSEPH HIBBS and FRANKEY ATKERSON, February 22, 1790. Consent of John
Adkison, father of Frankey.

JOHN HARDY and AHOLIBAMA HARDY, February 6, 1798. David Harris, surety.
Consent of Solomon Hardy for the marriage.

OVERSTREET HAIL and JUDITH WITT, October 22, 1792. John Witt, surety.

WILLIAM HOLT and LUCY SAUNDERS, December 28, 1785. David Saunders,
surety. Consent of Eliza Saunders.

WILLIAM HARRIS and NANCY HACKWORTH, April 15, 1799. Thomas Hackworth,
surety.

LABAN HAILE and MOLLEY HAILE, October 7, 1799. Robt. Woodcock, surety.
Consent of Stephen Haile, guardian of Molly.

MEAD HALE and BETSEY JACKSON, March 7, 1796. Thomas Jackson, surety.

THOMAS HOWELL and CLARY VAUGHN, November 12, 1795. John Philip Weaver,
surety. Consent of Joseph Vaughn, father of Clary.

MATTHEW HALL and MARY BANKS, December 29, 1794. Levi Best, surety.
Consent of Samuel Banks, father of Mary.

HENRY HARMAN and FANNY NEAL, June 9, 1789. William Neal, surety. Consent
of William Neal, father of Fanny.

HENRY HARRIS and SARAH WHITE, October 25, 1786. Jesse Reynolds, surety.
Consent of Sarah White, mother of Sarah.

JAMES HOWELL and LUCY RUSHER, October 21, 1795. George Rusher, surety.

JULIUS HATCHER and CELE FUQUA, September 2, 1799. Moses Fuqua, surety.
Consent of Thos. Fuqua, father of Cele.

HENRY HALL and SALLY HUGHES, March 5, 1785. Lance Woodward, surety.
Consent of Elizabeth Hughes, mother of Sally.

WILLIAM HARRIS and DOSHIA THORP, April 25, 1781. Bourne Price, surety.
Consent of Fran. Thorp, father of Doshia.

JACOB HARRIS and POLLEY OLDACRE, November 14, 1792. John Booram, surety.
Consent of John Oldacre, father of Polley.

FRANCIS HARRIS and NANCY THORP, September 6, 1796. William Harris, surety.

ENOCH HOGAN and ANN PERRIN, January 7, 1786. Charles Perrin, surety.
Consent of Milly Hogan, mother of Enoch; and consent of John
Perrin for the marriage of Ann.

GEORGE HUGHES and ELIZABETH ADAMS, March 29, 1783. Richard Roberts, surety.
Consent of Samuel Adams, the father of Elizabeth.

SIMON HUDSON and SALLY TRUEMAN, July 21, 1797. William Johnson, surety.

JEREMIAH HILTON and MARY HUDNALL, November 5, 1793.

BENJAMIN HODGES and FRANCES MITCHELL, August 24, 1783. Daniel Mitchell,
surety. Consent of Robt. Mitchell, Sr., father of Frances; and
consent of Rebecah Stevenson, guardian of Frances Mitchell.

RICHARD HAMBLETON and KITTY ANN FLIPPING, February 4, 1780. Joseph
Dickson, surety. Consent of Elizabeth Edwards, mother of Kitty
Ann Flippen.

JAMES HUDSON and LOUISA OWEN, August 19, 1797. John Owen, surety. Consent
of John and Margret Owen.

HENRY HAYNES, JR., batchelor, and BERSHEBA HAMPTON, spinster, March 22,
1768. Jno. Hampton, surety.

JOHN HUNT and ANN OWEN, May 6, 1793. Henry Sutphen, surety. Consent of
Owen Owen and Mary Owen.

ROBERT HAYNES and LUCY PHELPS, September 15, 1794. John Phelps, surety.

MOSES HARRIS and ELIZABETH MURRAY, January 16, 1781. David Murray, surety.

SAMUEL HOLT and ELIZABETH P. PRICE, March 7, 1791. Robert Wilson, surety. Consent of Robt. Price, father of Eliza. P. Price.

MATTHEW HARRIS and ELIZABETH TATE, May 8, 1764. Jesse Tate, surety. Consent of Henry Tate, father of Elizabeth.

JAMES HOWARD and ELIZABETH CHAPPELL, May 16, 1788. William Chappell, surety.

BAILEY HALLEY and SALLEY BAYMAN, February 1, 1793. Samuel Hally, surety. Certificate of Salley that she is of age.

CHARLES HARMAN and ELIZABETH NEAL, September 23, 1785. Frances Steel, surety. Consent of William Neal, father of Elizabeth.

WILLIAM HAIDEN and MARY LEMERT, January 25, 1795. Richard Shrewsbury, surety. Certificate of Mary saying she is of lawful age and that she has no parents in this State.

JONAH HOLE and ELIZABETH HOWELL, October 21, 1795. Stephen Potts and Israel Jarred, sureties. Certificate of Elizabeth that she is of age.

ALEX. HUNTER and MARTHA HAIRSTON, June 3, 1769. Hugh Hairston, surety. Consent of Robt. and Ruth Hairston.

BENJAMIN HADEN and MARTHA MOOREMAN, December 2, 1780. Jesse Mooreman, surety. Consent of Charles Mooreman, the father of Martha.

JOHN HALL and MOLLY WILLS, January 30, 1778. Euclid Wills, surety. Consent of Euclid Wills, father of Molly.

JOHN HOWELL and LAVINEY OAKS, December 22, 1795. Thomas Arthur, surety. Consent of Fanney Dixon, mother of Laviney.

WILLIAM HACKWORTH and DOROTHY NEWMAN, May 18, 1790. James Callaway, Jr., surety. Consent of the parent of Dorothy, the name is written in German.

JOHN HOPKINS and POLLY TURNER, September 1, 1800. Frazier Otey, surety.

WILLIAM HALL and USLY WOODWARD, November 25, 1777. Robt. Alexander, surety. Consent of Richard Woodward, father of Usly.

SAMUEL HATCHER and JULIA KENNEDY, October 26, 1789. Peter Forqurean, surety. Consent of Esther Kennedy.

JACOB HUNT and POLLY DOBYNS, January 14, 1800. Samuel Dobyns, surety.

JOSEPH HAWKINS and NANCY GILES, March 25, 1799. John Forqueran, surety. Consent of John Giles, father of Nancy, also states that she is of age.

PATRICK HOLLIGAN and FRANKEY HOWEL, November 25, 1793. John Howel, surety.

JOSEPH HUDDLESTON and SARAH GALLAWAY, April 19, 1791. Isham Gallaway,
    surety. Consent of John and Hannah Gallaway, parents of Sarah.

THOMAS HAYTH and MARTHA GILBERT, February 25, 1772. Wm. Manly, surety.
    Consent of Benj. Bilbert.

SAMUEL HENSLEY and SALLEY OWEN, November 23, 1795. James Hensley, surety.
    Consent of James Owen and Elizabeth Owen, parents of Salley.

WILLIAM INMAN and NANCY MORRIS, October 29, 1792. James Morris, surety.
    Consent of William Morrice.

ROBERT IRVIN and MARY SOUTH, November 4, _____(during the reign of George
    the Third) year is missing. John South, surety.

HARRY INNES and ELIZABETH CALLAWAY, October 7, 1775. Robt. Alexander,
    surety. Consent of James Callaway, father of Elizabeth.

DOUGLASS IRBY and HANNAH CANDLER, January 2, 1782. Archelous Moon, surety.
    Consent of John Canler, father of Hannah.

WILLIAM INGLIDUE and MAGDALEN ERWIN, July 21, 1794. James Byrens, surety.
    Certificate of Magdalen that she is of age, etc.

SOLOMON JONES and CENA NEWMAN, January 9, 1798. Franklin Creasey, surety.
    Consent of Nimrod Newman, the father of Cena.

JOSEPH JONES and BETSEY COATS, April 15, 1797. John Anthony, surety.
    Certificate of Betsey that she is 28 yrs. old.

WILLIAM JORDAN and LUCY STITH, June 15, 1780. John Mead, surety.
    Consent of Richard Stith.

WINSTON JORDAN and ELIZABETH MAYS, April 10, 1790. John Pate, surety.
    Consent of John Mays, father of Elizabeth.

JOHN JACKSON and FANNY DABNEY, July 19, 1790. John Jackson(S) surety.
    Consent of Rachel Dabney.

JULIUS JONES and RACHEL EADS, May 3, 1790. Isum Galloway, surety.
    Consent of Rachel herself.

THOMAS JONES and SUSANNA RAMSEY, December 23, 1786. Adam Young, surety.
    Certificate of Susanna that she is 23 years old.

JOHN JENNINGS and ANN CHILES, November 18, 1772. John Chiles, surety.

DAVID JONES and PATSEY NORTH, April 9, 1794. John North and Wm. North, sureties. Consent of Abraham North, the father of Patsey.

ISAAC JAMES and POLLY JAMES, November 24, 1796. David Martin, surety. Consent of Daniel and Susannah James, the parents of Polly.

WILLIAM JACKSON and NICEY HILL, October 26, 1784. Hezekiah Jackson, surety.

DANIEL JONES and ELIZABETH BRADFUTE, September 18, 1800. Robt. Bradfute, surety.

DAVID JONES of Charlotte County and SALLEY ANDERSON of Bedford County, March 6, 1783. William Anderson, surety. Consent of Jacob Anderson, father of Salley.

JACOB JAMES and NANCY BASHAM, December 24, 1792. Daniel James, surety.

PLEASANT JETER and JENNY HATCHER, December 15, 1800. Jeremiah Hatcher, surety. Consent of Jeremiah Hatcher, father of Jenny.

JOSEPH JARRETT and AGGY BEARD, October 23, 1780. George Simmons, surety. Consent of Margit Young, mother of Aggy Beard.

STEPHEN JONES and MARY GIBBS, December 28, 1782. Alex Gibbs, surety.

ISRAEL JARRED and ELIZABETH BROWN, January 27, 1794. Henry Preas, surety. Certificate of Elizabeth that she is of age.

JESSE JONES and BETSEY OWEN, October 9, 1797. James Owen, surety.

HENRY JONES and HANNAH COBB JACKSON, January 3, 1786. Isaac Cundiff, surety. Consent of Abel Jackson, father of Hannah.

JOHN DIETERICK JOS and MARY NEWMAN, November 1, 1785. Conrad Newman, surety.

LEWIS JONES and ELIZABETH BOCOCK, August 24, 1792. Philip Timberlake, surety. Consent of Elijah Bocock, father of Elizabeth.

JOSEPH JAMES and MARY McCAN, September 13, 1800. John McCan, surety.

JACOB JENKINS and NANCY VAUGHN, October 3, 1785. Martin Jones, surety. Consent of William Vaughn, father of Nancy.

JOHN JETER and POLLY HARDY, November 16, 1796. Joseph Hardy, surety.

DANIEL JAMES and ELIZABETH PRATT, September 24, 1792. John Pate, surety. Consent of John Pratt.

WILLIAM JENKINS and ANN JACKSON, November 22, 1779. Daniel Hammack, surety. Consent of Ann herself.

CHARLES JONES and FRANCES THORP, May 18, 1780. John Miller, surety. Consent of Frances herself and of B. Price.

BENJAMIN JOHNSON and AGNESS JOHNSON, March 23, 1778. Robt. Brooks, surety. Consent of Christopher Johnson, father of Agness.

JOHN JOHNSTON of Botetourt County and ELIZABETH BALLOW, September 1, 1783. Andrew Armstrong, surety. Consent of Ester Ballow, mother of Elizabeth.

BENJAMIN JOHNSON and REBECCA OLDAKER, December 7, 1794. John Oldaker, surety.

BENJAMIN JOHNSON and FRANCES HARDWICK, January 6, 1790. Pleasant Hardwick, surety. Consent of Elizabeth Hardwick.

JOHN JOHNSON and SUCKEY HACKWORTH, August 28, 1786. William Hackworth, surety.

JAMES JOHNSON and ANN COTTERILL, September 26, 1780. John Cottrell, surety.

JAMES JOHNSON and MILLY MOOREMAN, September 1, 1779. Zachariah Moorman, surety.

THOMAS JOHNSON and SALLY DICKERSON, October 26, 1795. Francis Dickerson, surety.

WILLIAM JONES and FANNY VAUGHAN, October 22, 1792. Martin Jones, surety.

WILLIAM JOHNSON and JOANNAH ARTHUR, November 1, 1786. Thomas Dixon, surety. Consent of Joseph Arthur, father of Joannah.

CHRISTOPHER JOHNSON and ELIZABETH HANCOCK, November 1, 1791. Samuel Hancock, surety.

JAMES JOHNSON and ELIZABETH SCARBOROUGH, October 22, 1785. Francis Burks, surety. Consent of Elizabeth herself.

MOORMAN JOHNSON and BETSY MOOREMAN, October 25, 1779. Joseph Johnson, surety. Consent of Micajah Moorman, the father of Betsey.

WILLIAM JOHNSON and DORCAS HOGAN, September 3, 1792. Enoch Hogan, surety.

JOSEPH JOHNSON and SARAH MOODY, September 7, 1796. Stephen Haile, surety.

JAMES KAY and MARY TOLLY, May 2, 1785. Alex Gibbs, Guy Smith, Caleb Tate, Wm. Quarles, Pratt Hughes, John Caffery, Wm. Whitten, and John Buford, sureties.

ZACHARIAH KENNETT and FRANKEY POLLARD, October 22, 1798. Harris Toney, surety.

THOMAS KEENEY and MARY REAVES, September 9, 1778. Joseph Cogwell, surety. Consent of John Reaves, father of Mary.

JOB KERNS and PHEBE CLARKE, December 31, 1800. Isham Clark, surety.

WILLIAM KING and BETTY BROWN, February 26, 1788. James King, surety.
Consent of Betty and Zachariah Brown.

PETER KENNETT and MILLY BLANKENSHIP, October 26, 1789. Benj. Blankenship,
surety. Consent of William and Elizabeth Blankenship.

ALEXANDER KASEY and SUSANNAH SHAON, July 25, 1791. David Hughes, surety.
Certificate of Susannah, stating that her parents are not alive.

JOHN KENNETT and UNITY BLANKENSHIP, November 24, 1789. Benj. Blankenship,
surety. Consent of William and Elizabeth Blankenship.

GEORGE KEY and SUCKEY CRAGHEAD, August 22, 1785. Robert Cowan, surety.
Consent of John Craghead, father of Suckey.

JAMES KERR and RUTH GADDY, December 13, 1783. Bartholomew Gaddy, surety.
Consent of George Gaddy, father of Ruth.

ALEXANDER KERR and KATHARINE CLARK, February 4, 1792. Isham Clark, surety.

MICHAEL KELLY and MARY THOMPSON, April 26, 1772. Thomas Bruce, surety.

GEORGE KEY and IZBELL KENNEDY, November 14, 1785. James Kasey, surety.
Consent of William Kennedy, father of Izbell.

THOMAS KERR and MARTHA McCLANAHAN, May 1, 1786. Nathaniel Kerr, surety.
Consent of Thomas McClannahan, father of Martha.

GEORGE KINZER and ELIZABETH MAYBERRY, May 4, 1797. Henry Mayberry, surety.

JAMES KEENUM and ELIZABETH MASON, widow, March 12, 1785. Richard Dale,
surety.

JAMES KELLEY and SARAH ARNOLD, May 10, 1779. Richard Elam, surety.
Certificate of Sarah that she is of age.

BENJAMIN KING and ELENDER COLE, September 15, 1792. Avery King, surety.
Consent of Avary King and Nany King, Francis Cole and Mary Cole,
parents.

THOMAS KENWORTHY and NANCY SYNOR, March 4, 1799. John Synor, surety.

GEORGE KENNEDY and CHRISTIANA WARNER, April 16, 1800. Jacob Shepherd,
surety. Certificate of Christiana that she is of age.

DAVID KESSON and ELIZABETH CRUM, October 11, 1796. Thomas Cadwalader,
surety. Certificate of Elizabeth that she is of age.

JOHN KERN and ANNA PATTERSON, October 19, 1793. William Patterson,
surety.

JAMES KAY and KATY DOOLEY, November 20, 1798. Thomas Dooley, surety.

JACOB KENT and MARY CROCKETT, April 5, 1760. Joseph Crockett, surety.

DENNIS KNOX and KEZIAH LAWSON, June 3, 1789. Henry Townshend, surety. Certificate that Keziah is of age.

JACOB KRANTZ and SARAH ARTHUR, December 16, 1791. Benj. Arthur, surety. Consent of Thomas Arthur, Jr., father of Sarah.

MARTIN KING, JR., and ANN DENNIS, September 13, 1784. Elisha Dennis, surety. Consent of Elizabeth Haynes, the mother of Ann Dennis.

WILLIAM KENT and MARY COCK, March 11, 1773. John Cocke, surety. Consent of George Cock, father of Mary.

WILLIAM KASEY and HANNAH NEWLON, December 27, 1798. Alexander Kasey, surety. Consent of John Newlon, father of Hannah.

LUKE KENT and JOHN COCK, January 8, 1782. John Cock, surety.

WILLIAM KERR and LURENA WORLEY, August 28, 1781. Wm. Geddy, surety.

NATHANIEL KERR and MARY PARISH, April 23, 1792. Wm. Kerr, surety.

JEREMIAH KIRTLY and MARY ROBINSON, June 22, 1773. Jacob Early, surety. Consent of Mary herself.

JOSEPH KENNETT and IZABELL AYRES, June 2, 1792. William White, surety. Consent of John and Catharan Kennett, also of John and Nanny Ayres.

JOHN KING and JENNY EUBANKS, September 1, 1798. Lain Jones, surety. Consent of Ambrose Eubank, father of Jenny.

JOHN KINZER and POLLY DEARDORF, May 6, 1797. Jacob Waggoner, surety.

CHARLES KERN and HANNAH KERN, November 13, 1793. Thomas Kern, surety. Consent of Michael Kern, father of Hannah.

GEORGE KEY and MARY SENTER, October 14, 1782. Zachariah Davis, surety.

ABRAHAM KARN and BETSEY FREDERICK, August 3, 1798. Michael Frederick, surety.

GEORGE KERN and BARBARA KERN, January 22, 1787. Henry Mayberry, surety. Consent of Elizabeth Kern, the mother of Barbara.

.

ROBERT LANCASTER and NANCY KING, February 21, 1792. John Lancaster, surety. Consent of Avra King, mother of Nancy.

HENRY LANE, JR. and SUSANNAH DOUGLASS, January 8, 1800. Geo. Douglass, surety. Consent of Henry Lane, Sr., the father of Henry, Jr.

AUGUSTINE LEFTWICH and ELIZABETH STOVALL, December 2, 1779. Thomas Fuqua, surety.

EDWARD LUSTER and BARBARA HARMAN, October 11, 1785. Daniel Neule, surety. Consent of Peter Harman, father of Barbara.

JAMES LEFTWICH and MATILDA CALLAWAY, November 20, 1797. Archibald Page, Jr., surety. Consent of Wm. Callaway, father of Matilda.

CHRISTOPHER LYNCH, batchelor and ANNE WARD, spinster, October 15, 1765. John McConnel, surety. Consent of John Ward, father of Anne.

JOHN LYNCH, batchelor, and MARY BOWLES, spinster, August ___, 177__ (before 1776). Robert Clark, surety.

DAVID LYONS and ELIZABETH HILL, April 7, 1785. Charles Jones, surety. Consent of Elizh. Hill, mother of Elizabeth; also of Stephen Lyons, father of David.

BEVERLEY LEE and REBECCA LEE, October 15, 1799. Garnett Lee, surety. Consent of William Lee, father of Rebecca.

FRANCIS LEE and NANCY BOWCOCK, November 14, 1791. Elijah Bowcok, surety.

WILLIAM LOWRY, JUNR. and NANCY HOWARD, December 17, 1796. Thomas Lowry, surety. Consent of David Saunders, Guardian of Nancy. Her father was William Howard, deceased.

JOHN LONG, batchelor, and MARY HAINES, August 3, 1772. Stephen Saunders, surety. Consent of Mary herself.

THOMAS LUMPKIN and LUCY BRAMBLETT, March 4, 1778. Robert Alexander, surety.

WILLIAM LONG and MASSAY WHEAT, December 7, 1795. Zadack Wheat, surety.

GEORGE LEWIS and NANCY YOUNG, Frebruary 19, 1790. John Young, surety.

DANIEL LAWHORN and SARAH SWAIN, February 11, 1797. Charles Swain, surety.

_____ _____, and ELIZABETH LOWRY, August 27, 1771. Nathaniel Nance, surety. Wm. Lowry, guardian of Elizabeth.

FARRISS LAYNE and REBECCA FARISS, August 17, 1790. James Rather, surety. Certificate of Rebeccah, herself.

BURWELL LOGWOOD and PRUEY PEYTON, July 19, 1794. Gross Scruggs, surety. Certificate of Pruey that she is of age.

THOMAS LUMPKIN and ANN BRAMBLETT, October 25, 1798. William Bramblett, surety.

CHARLES LYNCH, JR. and SALLY ADAMS, October 20, 1777. James Adams, surety. Consent of Robt. Adams, father of Sally.

THOMAS LOWRY and ELIZABETH WILLIAMS, October 18, 1794. Jeremiah Lockett, surety. Consent of John and Margot Williams, also states Elizabeth is of age.

JOHN LANE and ELIZA WILLIAMS, December 25, 1780. Robert Williams, surety.

AUGUSTINE LEFTWICH, JR., batchelor, and MARY TURNER, spinster, February 12, 1765. Consent of Richard Turner, father of Mary. Gross Scruggs, surety.

THOMAS LANE and NANCY DABNEY, August 5, 1783. James Hurt, surety. Consent of Cornelius Dabney, father of Nancy.

WILLIAM LUSH and MARY DOOLEY, November ___, 1781. William Downing, surety.

JOHN LAVINDER and ELIZABETH ALLEN, (date blank, James Wood is Governor). John Allen and Robert Witt, sureties.

ELISHA LYON and RHODA HATCHER, July 11, 1792. Zedekiah Hatcher, surety. Consent of Farley Hatcher, brother of Rhoda.

ELIJAH LYON and SALLY FINNEY, July 10, 1798. John Finney, surety. Consent of Peter Finney.

BURLEY LACEY and JUDITH BROWN, February 9, 1786. William Woody, surety. Consent of Thomas Brown.

JABEZ LEFTWICH and DELILAH STOVALL, February 1, 1785. Augustin Leftwich, surety.

LITTLEBERRY LEFTWICH and FANNY HOPKINS, June 13, 1778. Francis Hopkins, surety.

WILLIAM LEFTWICH and RUTH AYRES, December 22, 1795. William Richardson, surety. Consent of James Ayres, the father of Ruth.

JOHN LOWRY and ABIGAIL ELLIOTT, December 12, 1792. William Elliott, surety.

WILLIAM LEFTWICH, JR. and FRANCES OTEY, June 16, 1788. Isaac Otey, surety. Consent of W. Leftwich.

THOMAS LEWIS and AGNESS JONES, December 28, 1781. Archelaus Moon, surety. Consent of Agness herself.

PEYTON LEFTWICH and MILLY FUQUA, December 24, 1793. John Pate, surety. Consent of Thomas Fuqua, father of Milly.

PHILIP LETSINGER and ANN PETTIT, July 27, 1789. David Mayberry, surety. Consent of Lewis Pettit.

JOHN LEFTWICH and SUSANNA SMITH, February 5, 1788. David Saunders, surety. Consent of Ann Smith, mother of Susanna.

THOMAS LEFTWICH and JANE STRATTON, October 27, 1783. Henry Saunders, surety.

ISHAM LAWHORN and NANCY HACKWORTH, September 13, 1799. Francis Wood, surety. Consent of Jas. Hackworth, father of Nancy.

WILLIAM B. LYTLE and POLLY HUNT, December 23, 1799. William Creasey, surety. Consent of Elizabeth Hunt, the mother of Polly.

CHRISTOPHER LANDES and ELIZABETH ROBINSON, May 13, 1799. John Robinson, surety. Consent of Samuel Landes, father of Christopher.

JAMES LEFTWICH and MILLEY TURNER, August 2, 1797. Joel Leftwich, surety. Consent of Admire Turner, and also consent of Augustine Leftwich.

JESSE LEFTWICH and DOSHIA TRIGG, July 20, 1791. Stephen Trigg, surety. Consent of John Trigg, father of Doshia.

JOSIAH LOCKETT and JENCY JETER, January 14, 1793. Pleasant Jeter, surety. Consent of Henry Jeter, father of Jency.

JOEL LEFTWICH and NANCY TURNER, December 24, 1781. John Leftwich, surety. Consent of D. Wright for the marriage of the above parties.

JESSE LOCKETT and MARY PALMORE, December 22, 1792. Jesse Reynolds, surety. Consent of Benjamin Palmore, the father of Mary.

WILLIAM McCOY and JOANNA PAYNE, August 16, 1781. Littleberry Hurt, surety. Consent of Frail Paine, brother of Joanna.

JOHN MULLINS and MILLY HACKWORTH, August 26, 1793. Joseph Hackworth, surety.

MOSES MILAM and EDY FUQUA, September 28, 1790. Joseph Fuqua, surety. Consent of Anny Milam, mother of Moses. Also consent of John Fuqua, father of Edy.

THOMAS MURRAY and SUSANNA SCOTT, September 26, 1785. Gross Scruggs, surety. Consent of Susanna herself, and also of William Scott, her brother.

JAMES MURPHY and MARGARETT HILL, November 28, 1796. Isaac Thomas, surety. Consent of John and Elizabeth Hill, the parents of Margarett. She is 16 years old.

THOMAS McREYNOLDS and LUCY DABNEY, November 3, 1781. John Mead, surety. Consent of Anna Dabney, mother of Lucy.

JAMES MORRICE and POLLY INMAN, August 6, 1792. John Morrice, surety. Consent of William Inman, father of Polly.

ROBERT McFARLAND and MARY JONES, April 3, 1778. Robert Stevens, surety. Consent of Mary herself.

ANDERSON MELTON and NANCY RICHARDSON, November 26, 1787. Joseph Richardson, surety.

JAMES MITCHELL (Clerk) and FRANCES RICE, December 19, 1782. John Mitchell, surety. Consent of David Rice, the father of Frances.

OBEDIAH MOORE and AGGY COWHARD, April 23, 1798. Reuben Cowhard, surety.

MICAJAH MILAM and MARGARETT NEALE, September 8, 1788. William Wright, surety. Consent of Daniel Neal, father of Margarett.

NED MOSS and RACHEL HILL, July 20, 1793. Robert Hill, surety. Consent of Rachel herself.

LEWIS MASON and BETSEY DALE, February 1, 1792. Reuben Mason, surety. Consent of Richard and Mary Dale, the parents of Betsey.

THOMAS MILLICAN and MILLE ROUTON, June 28, 1780. William Mullican, surety. Consent of Richard Routon, father of Mille.

JOHN MEARS and ANN BURNETT, November 26, 1798. Elisha Burnett, surety. Consent of Elisha Burnett.

SAMUEL MITCHELL and PEGGY CLAYTOR, September 1, 1791. Samuel Claytor, surety. Consent of Samuel Claytor; Peggy is of age.

WILLIAM MILAM and SUSANNA HILLEY, March 15, 1793. Matthew Worley, surety. Certificate of Susanna that she is of age.

RUSH MILAM and ELIZABETH FOWLER, July 16, 1783. James Wilson, surety. Consent of William Fowler, father of Elizabeth.

SAMUEL MAYS and AGNESS WRIGHT, October 22, 1792. John Pate, surety. Consent of Joseph Wright, father of Agness.

MOSES MAHEW and NANCY TURNER, December 27, 1796. John Gordon, surety. Certificate of Nancy that she has agreed to the marriage.

WILLIAM McINTIRE and SUSANNAH LUELLIN, August 8, 1789. Champy Wilson, surety. Certificate of Sukey, asking that license be granted.

JAMES McDAVITT and ANNA REID, June 30, 1794. John Patrick, surety.

ALEXANDER MAHEW and LYDDA THURMAN, November 23, 1795. Joseph Thurman, surety.

STEPHEN MITCHELL and KITTY WADE, March 8, 1783. Isaac Wade, surety.

JOHN MURPHY and RUTH MILAM, February 18, 1797. Solomon Milam, surety.

JOSEPH MOORE and SALLY HARRIS, February 25, 1799. Boyce Eidson, surety.

THOMAS McCORMACK and NANCY DURRETT, August 1, 1795. Anderson McCormack, surety.

JAMES McFARLAND and MARGARET DOWNING, September 13, 1763. John Downing, surety.

DENNIS McCORMACK and MARY MEADOR, May 18, 1791. Micajah Dowell, surety. Consent of Jeremiah Meador, the father of Mary.

JAMES McELROY of Prince Edward County and MARGARET IRVIN, of Bedford County, October 11, 1770. Robert Irvin, surety. Consent of John Irvin, father of Margaret.

GABRIEL MINOR and EDITH WHITE RICE, March 11, 1793. Ben Rice, surety.

ACQUILLA MITCHELL and SUSANNAH BURGIS, August 23, 1790. John Mitchell, Jr., surety. Consent of Susannah Burgis, also signed by Elijah Mitchell.

ADAM McCORMACK and BETT, a free Negro Woman, late the property of John Murphy, September 22, 1794. John Ayers, surety.

JOSEPH MARTIN and NANCY HUNTER, September 1, 1780. Thomas Martin, surety.

BENJAMIN MORLAND and KEZIAH HARVY, September 6, 1794. Evan Harvy, surety.

NATHANIEL MORRIS, batchelor, and ANN MORRIS, spinster, July 28, 1772. Samuel Morris, surety.

NICHOLAS MEAD and MARY BATES, January 18, 1779. Alexr. Gibbs, surety. Consent of Mary herself.

THOMAS MARTIN and ELIZABETH SLINKER, November 18, 1799. John Slinker, surety.

BENJAMIN MEAD and ELIZABETH BROWN, December 26, 1796. John Leftwich, surety. Consent of Daniel Brown, father of Elizabeth.

JOHN McCLENACHAN and MARY DAWSON, February 10, 1780. Elisha Williams, surety. Consent of John Dawson (spelt Dosin), father of Mary.

JOHN McNEIL and MARY OVERSTREET, January 23, 1786. Daniel Lockett, surety. Consent of James Overstreet, the father of Mary.

HENRY MAYBERRY and MAGDALENE CARN, April 2, 1778. Michael Carn, surety.

WILLIAM McGEHEE and CHARLOTTE GILLIAM, December 12, 1791. George Steele, surety. Consent of Richard Gilliam, father of Charlotte.

BENJAMIN MUSGROVE and KEZIA HALL, December 15, 1796. Elisha Hall, surety. Consent of Magdalean Hall, mother of Kezia.

WILLIAM MOSELEY and NANCY IRVINE, December 1, 1784. Robert Cowan, surety.

ROBERT MITCHELL and MARY WITT, April 16, 1799. William Crouch, surety.

ALLEN MELTON and ANN WILKS, January 25, 1787. John Cooper, surety.

JOHN MILLER and SUSANNA ANDERSON, September 22, 1783. Reuben Slaughter, surety.

JOHN MERRITT, JR. and RHODA MERRITT, February 18, 1795. Pleasant Magann, surety. Consent of John Merritt, father of John, Jr.

HENRY MILLER and SARAH PEARCY, December 4, 1780. Stephen Dooley, surety. Consent of John and Marg. Pearcy, parents of Sarah.

JACOB MOORMAN and KATY GROOM, March 3, 1800. Jonathan Groom, surety.

WILLIAM MEADOR and NANCY ELLAGE, April 3, 1787. William Board, surety. Consent of Nancy Yeats, mother of Nancy Ellage; and consent of Jeremiah Meador, father of William.

ARTHUR MARKHAM and MARTHA HILL, widow, May 2, 1792. Lewis Speece, surety.

BENJAMIN MEADOR and ELIZABETH BASHAM, December 21, 1796. Jesse Hix, surety. Consent of William Basham, the father of Elizabeth.

THOMAS MOORE and NANCY WALKER, January 9, 1788. John Claytor, surety. Consent of Sam'l Walker, father of Nancy.

SAMUEL MITCHELL and SINER PULLEN, December 16, 1785. Daniel Mitchell, surety. Consent of Thos. Pullen, father of Siner; also states she is of age.

ARTHUR MOSELEY and NANCY TRIGG, November 24, 1777. Robert Alexander, surety. Consent of Mary Trigg, mother of Nancy.

JEHU MEADOR and NANCY BOARD, September 1, 1796. Jason Meador, surety. Consent of John Board, father of Nancy.

JAMES McCLASKEY and MARY ANN THOMS, April 10, 1793. Robert Scott, surety. Certificate of Mary Ann, stating that she is of age.

JEHU MEADOR and NANCY WRIGHT, September 2, 1793. John Pate, surety. Consent of Joseph Wright, father of Nancy.

ISAAC MITCHELL and PRETHA MITCHELL, January 29, 1788. Edward Burgess, surety. Consent of John Mitchell, Senr., the father of Isaac. Also consent of Prethia.

JESSE MITCHELL and MARJORY RATLIFF, August 24, 1779. Thomas McReynolds, surety. Consent of Jas. Ratliff, the father of Marjory.

ABRAHAM MAYBERRY and ANN WOMAX, March 11, 1794. Jacob Mayberry, surety. Consent of Sarah Womax, mother of Ann.

PETER MASTIN and JEMIMA GADDEY, November 9, 1790. Joseph Gadde, surety. Consent of Joseph Gadde, and of Jemima.

JOHN McCABE and SUSANNAH MOZELEY, September 6, 1792. Henry Brown, surety. Consent of Walter Mozeley, father of Susannah.

SIMON MAJOR and ABIGAL WEST, December 28, 1798. Joseph West, surety.

JAMES MARKHAM and SABRINA REYNOLDS, January 29, 1787. Jesse Reynolds, surety.

DANIEL McNEIL and SARAH COOPER, October 10, 1786. Dabney Cooper, surety.
Consent of Arthur Cooper, father of Sarah.

HENRY MEREDITH and MARY EPPS COBBS, August 30, 1800. Washington Lambeth,
surety. Consent of Mary herself.

JOHN MENZIES and MARY IRVINE, December 2, 1774. James Steptoe, surety.
Consent of Robt. Cowan for the above marriage.

DAVID MAYBERRY and BETSEY GILPIN, December 28, 1789. Francis Green
Gilpin, surety.

CHARLES McGLOCKLIN, JUNR., and ELIZABETH ASBERRY, November 18, 1777.
Chas. McGlocklin, Senr., surety. Consent of Thomas Asberry,
father of Elizabeth.

IRA MEADOR and SARAH WINFREY, May 23, 1791. Lewis Turner, surety.

MICHAEL McNEELY and AGNESS WOODS, February ___, 1769. William Boyd,
surety.

ALEXANDER MOORE and JENNY EARLY, November 17, 1781. Jeremiah Early,
surety.

SAMUEL MARTIN and MARY KASEY, November 25, 1799. Alexander Kasey, surety.
Consent of James Kasey, father of Mary; also of William Martin.

MICAJAH McCORMACK and SARAH BARKER, May 29, 1798. Edward Barker, surety.

MOSES MILAM and ELIZABETH BOYD, October 19, 1774. Moses Dooley, surety.
Certificate of William Boyd, father of Elizabeth, stating that
she is of age.

JOHN McGEHEE and MOURNING ADAMS, October 20, 1777. James Adams, surety.
Consent of Robt. Adams, father of Mourning.

BENJAMIN McFARLAND and MARY BLACKBURN, October 7, 1777. John McFarland,
surety. Consent of Andrew Blackburn, the father of Mary.

BENJAMIN MITCHELL and POLLY BOWYER, November 23, 1789. John Mitchell,
surety.

RHODES MEADE and PRISCILLA NEWLON, November 17, 1800. Jonathan Cundiff,
surety. Consent of James Newlon, father of Priscilla.

JOSEPH MORLAN and KATY LOYD, July 25, 1796. Henry Loyd, surety.

JACOB MOON and MARTHA GILBERT, June 16, 1778. Robert Alexander, surety.

JOSEPH McMURTRY and SUSANNA PATTEN, August 27, 1759. William Manley,
surety.

JOHN MILLAM and DITSEY REYNOLDS, November 7, 1799. Joel Salmons, surety.
Consent of John Reynolds, father of Ditsey.

JACOB MABERRY and RODY WOMAX, February 27, 1790. David Mayberry, surety.

RICHARD MEADOR and SARAH YATES, May 18, 1791. Micajah Dowell, surety. Consent of Jane Yates, mother of Sarah.

JOHN MAY and ELIZABETH HUNTER, April 19, 1779. John Hunter, Jr., surety. Consent of John Hunter, father of Elizabeth.

JACOB MORRIS and SALLY CANADA, May 12, 1797. George Welsh, surety. Consent of Geo. Canada, father of Sally.

JOHN MILLER and MARY JOHNSON (widow), June 6, 1771. Isham Talbot, surety. Consent of Mary Johnson, herself.

THOMAS MARKHAM and NELLY WILKERSON, Decmeber 3, 1785. Parson Wilkerson, surety. Consent of Joseph Wilkerson, father of Nelly.

ABRAHAM MORGAN and PATTY DEAREN, March 2, 1793. Mordecai Morgan, surety. Consent of John Dearen, father of Patty.

LAWRENCE McGEORGE and NANCY SMITH, September 22, 1775. Robt. Alexander, surety. Certificate from John Hook, stating that Nancy is daughter of John Smith, etc., and that her brothers John and Guy are willing, etc.

JOHN MORRIS and SUSANNA JOHNSON, October 16, 1786. Nicholas Osburn, surety. Consent of William Johnson, the father of Susanna.

WILLIAM MILLER and BETSEY NORTH, April 11, 1785. Benjamin Robinson, surety. Consent of Abram North, father of Betsey.

GEORGE MOODY and MARY HUGHES, November 8, 1786. Philip Sanders, surety. Consent of Rese and Lucy Hughes, parents of Mary.

JACOB MILLER and SUSANNAH ABSTON, August 20, 1800. Mathew Lynch, surety. Consent of Joshua Abston, father of Susannah.

CHARLES MOOREMAN and MARY BRANCH, August 28, 1781. Littleberry Leftwich, surety. Consent of Mary herself.

JOSEPH McGUIRE and MARY SCARBOROUGH, March 27, 1786. Lawrence McGuire, surety.

WILLIAM McCORMACK and JUDITH WRIGHT, January 3, 1791. Micajah McCormack, surety. Consent of Joseph Wright, the father of Judith.

JAMES MOORMAN and ELIZABETH PAYNE, September 2, 1799. Anderson McCormack, surety. Consent of John and Sara Payne, parents of Elizabeth.

THOMAS MILLAM and LUCY LANGSDON, August 1, 1791. William Shepherd, surety. Certificate of Lucy saying that she is of age.

JOHN McGINNIS and MARY HUSTON, April 10, 1784. James Huston, surety. Consent of Thomas and Agnes Huston, the parents of Mary.

ROLAND MAJORS and ELIZABETH STANDLEY, October 16, 1795. Wm. Hix, surety. Consent of Elizabeth herself.

WILLIAMSON MILLNER and SALLY NOELL, January 24, 1792. Sovereign Jeter, surety. Certificate of Sally that she is of age.

SAMUEL MERRITT and ELINOR RHINE, December 23, 1799. Peter Follis, surety. Consent of Elinor herself.

REUBEN MASON and CATY RICHARDSON, February 22, 1790. John Board, surety. Consent of Margaret Richardson, mother of Caty.

WILSON McKENNY and ELIZABETH STEVENS, March 27, 1780. Robert Stevens, surety.

JOB MEADOR and PATTEY WOOD, November 17, 1785. William Martin, surety. Consent of Peter Wood, father of Pattey.

ROB. MARTIN, JUNR., and MARY THOMPSON, January ___, 1762. Bond is torn, and name of surety is missing.

ELIJAH MITCHELL and JUDITH KEY, December 7, 1789. John Key, surety.

SAMUEL MURPHY and POLLEY LEFTWICH, January 14, 1799. Uriah Leftwich, Jr., surety. Consent of Uriah Leftwich, the father of Polly. Also consent of J. Murphy, father of Samuel.

MORDICA MORGAN and ELIZABETH NICKOLS, January 28, 1791. Morgan Morgan, surety. Consent of Bazdel Nichols, father of Elizabeth.

JOHN MURPHY, JR., and THEODOSHA TURNER, December 30, 1799. Elijah Turner, surety. Consent of Elijah Turner, father of Theodosha.

LAWRENCE McGEORGE and MARY PATE, October 26, 1795. Lewis Squires, surety. Consent of Mathew Pate, father of Mary.

JOHN MOBLY and ELIZABETH FRAIR, December 30, 1779. Samuel Woodward, surety.

JOHN McGLOTHLIN and RHODA FUQUA, September 22, 1778. Henry Fuqua, surety.

THOMAS McGLAUCHLIN and ELIZABETH GASH, April 1, 1786. Alexander Gibbs, surety.

WILLIAM MORGAN and SARAH INMAN, February 23, 1792. Morgan Morgan, surety. Consent of William and Susanna Inman, parents of Sarah.

JOHN McGLOTHLIN and ELIZABETH PERRIN, October 15, 1798. Charles Perrin, surety.

EZEKIEL MORRIS and MARY THURMOND, August 18, 1770. Isham Talbot, surety. Consent of Mary herself.

SIMON MILLER, JUNR., and ELIZABETH READ, September 29, 1779. Zach. Callaway, surety. Consent of W. Read, father of Elizabeth.

JOHN MITCHELL and ELIZABETH HARDWICK, December 29, 1783. Jeremiah Taylor, surety. Consent of Robert Hardwick, father of Elizabeth.

ARCHELAUS MOON and ANN ANDERSON, December 29, 1784. Robert Anderson, surety.

RICHARD MERRITT and NANCY HUNTER, February 14, 1788. Peter Hunter, surety. Consent of Thomas Merritt, father of Richard.

WILLIAM MOODY and SALLEY HAILE, February 18, 1792. Robert Woodcock, surety. Consent of Stephen and Nancy Haile, parents of Salley.

ARTHUR MOSELEY and PAMELIA CRUMP, May 10, 1799. Caleb Tate, Jr., surety.

MORDECAI McLAIN and ANNEY DABNEY, November 24, 1800. James Turner, surety. Consent of Mary Dabney, mother of Anney.

IGNATIUS MITCHELL and SARAH MITCHELL, December 15, 1792. Isaac Mitchell, surety. Consent of John and Ann Mitchell.

NED MATTHEWS and NANCY CARTER, 5th _____, 1794. John _____, surety. Cannot make out last name of surety.

SAMUEL MOODY and RUTH CADWALADER, April 13, 1799. Stephen Martin, surety.

JOHN MALONE and MARY ANN POSEY, July 20, 1780. Mesheck Hicks, surety. Request of Robt. Fitzhugh that license be issued.

JOHN MURPHY and KATY BATES, April 25, 1770. William Bates, surety.

JOHN McCLUNEY and ISABELLA SHEARER, July 26, 1779. William McCluney, surety.

STEPHEN MARTIN and ELIZABETH DOBYNS, December 1, 1794. John McGlothlan, surety.

PATRICK NENNEY and LUCY BRAMBLETT, June 20, 1796. William Bramblett, surety. Consent of Anna Bramblett, mother of Lucy.

GARRETT NEWMAN and ELIZABETH DIXON, October 29, 1791. Edmund Franklin, surety. Consent of Conrad Newman; also states that John Dixon is the father of Elizabeth.

WILLIAM NANCE and MARY HOWARD, March 3, 1784. Thomas Nance, surety.

DAVID NIMMO and JENNY BLACK, October 24, 1796. Andrew Black, surety.

ARCHIBALD NANCE and NANCY WILLIAMS, March 10, 1794. Isaac Wade, surety. Consent of Roger Williams, father of Nancy.

CORNELIUS NOELL and NANCY MILLNER, December 31, 1798. Henry Jeter, surety.

BAZDELL NICHOLS, JR. and CLARISSA CANNON, March 25, 1799. Leroy Meador, surety. Consent of William Cannon, father of Clarissa.

THOMAS NICHOLS and NANCY PAYNE, October 22, 1798. Joshua Kennett, surety. Consent of William and Amy Payne.

JESSE NICHOLS and SALLY FIELDS, October 27, 1800. John Fields, surety.

HENRY NEWMAN and MARY ARTHUR, January 28, 1788. Samuel Wilks, surety. Consent of Thomas Arter, father of Mary; also of Conrad Newman.

EDWARD NIX and ELIZABETH PRICE, January 15, 1790. John Williamson, surety. Consent of Daniel Price, father of Elizabeth.

ARCHIBALD NICHOLS and JUDITH HATCHER, December 10, 1792. Ward Hatcher, surety. Consent of Richard Hatcher, father of Judith.

ARCHIBALD NICHOLS and SARAH WOOLINGTON, November 25, 1779. John Payne, surety.

FLAIL NICHOLS and ANN HATCHER, January 4, 1780. Patrick Lynch, surety. Certificate from Ann herself.

WILLIAM NEEL and EMILIA NEEL, August 5, 1793. Alexr. Gibbs, surety. Consent of Walter Neel, father of Emilia.

PHILPOT NICHOLS and MARY McCOY, March 6, 1800. Thomas Payne, surety. Consent of William Maccoy, father of Mary.

JOHN NEAL and PATTY GIBBS, January 1, 1783. Alexr. Gibbs, surety.

DANIEL NEAL and SALLY CALLAWAY, June 3, 1793. Andrew Steal, surety. Consent of James and Susana Hilton, parents of Sally Callaway.

DANIEL NEAL and POLLY BOOTHE, August 12, 1790. William Boothe, surety.

WILLIAM NEAL and SUSANNA NEAL, June 22, 1789. Samuel Hatcher, surety. Consent of William and Rachel Neal.

ADAM NEWMAN and MARY DIXON, November 23, 1795. Henry Newman, surety. Consent of John and Mary Dixson, parents of Mary.

ZACHARIAH NEAL and ANNA NEAL, November 29, 1796. Robert Goodman, surety. Consent of Zachariah Neal, father of Anna.

DAVID NORTH and ELIZABETH RUCKER, January 6, 1785. Abraham North, surety.

JAMES NABORS and NANCY BANDY, March 12, 1791. George Bandy, surety. Consent of Richard Bandy, father of Nancy.

ARTHUR NEWMAN and LUCY CREASEY, October 5, 1793. Franklin Creasey, surety. Consent of Thos. Creasey, father of Lucy.

JAMES NEWMAN and SARAH RICHARDSON, May 9, 1798. John Richardson, surety. Consent of Joseph Richardson, father of Sarah.

WILLIAM NICHOLS and PHEBE JOHNSON, December 28, 1786. Morgan Morgan, surety. Certificate of Phebe that she is of full age and consents.

WILLIAM NORTH and POLLY CALLAWAY, June 8, 1781. Lance Woodward, surety. Consent of Sarah Brown, mother of Polly Callaway.

ELISHA NICHOLS and NANCY PAYNE, July 24, 1797. John Nichols, surety.

JOHN NICHOLS and SARAH PAYNE, September 29, 1784. Wm. McCoy, surety.

JESSE OWEN and ELIZABETH BROOKS, December 27, 1773. Robert Brooks, surety.

NICHOLAS OSBURN and RACHEL HIBBS, January 11, 1786. Solomon Butler, surety. Consent of Isaac Hibbs, father of Rachel; and of John Osburn, father of Nicholas.

THORNTON O'NEAL and ELIZABETH FOSTER, October 15, 1792. James Foster, surety. Consent of James Foster, Senr., father of Elizabeth.

JACOB O'NEAL and MARY STEEL, April 27, 1789. Walter o'Neal and Sol. Tracy, sureties. Consent of Francis Steal, father of Mary.

JOHN O'NEAL and POLLY FOSTER, February 11, 1792. James Foster, surety. Consent signed by Thornton O'Neal and James Foster.

ISAAC OLDAKERS and HANNAH BOORAM, August 16, 1791. John Booram, surety. Consent of Aaron Booram, the father of Hannah.

JOHN H. OTEY and BETSEY BUFORD, March 29, 1790. Chas. Caffery, surety. Consent of Henry Buford, father of Betsey.

SAMUEL OWEN and ELIZABETH LYNCH, January 22, 1792. John Owen, surety. Consent of John and Mary Lynch, parents of Elizabeth.

PHILIP OWEN and URSLY BROOKS, April 25, 1770. Robert Brooks, surety.

BARNETT (BERNARD) OWEN and JUDITH PALMER, December 17, 1790. Joseph Hardy. Consent of Ben. Palmore, father of Judith.

THOS. OLIVER, batchelor, and AGNESS BOYD, spinster, June 26, 1764. William Boyd, surety.

FRAZIER OTEY and MILDRED LEFTWICH, November 20, 1793. Chas. Caffery, surety. Consent of W. Leftwich, father of Mildred.

SAMUEL OSBURN and MARY McGLOTHLEN, December 31, 1788. Robert Dollar, surety. Consent of John Osburn and John MacClohlon, fathers of the parties.

JOHN OVERSTREET and NANCY PHILIPS, October 4, 1797. William Shoemaker, surety. Certificate from Nancy herself.

JOHN OVERSTREET and NANCY DABNEY, November 3rd, 1785. George Dabney, surety. Consent of Cornelius Dabney, father of Nancy.

RICHARD OGLESBY and MARY STAPLES, February 1, 1775. Thomas Oglesby, surety. Consent of Samuel Staples, the father of Mary.

JAMES OVERSTREET and RUTH HURT, September 13, 1799. Henry Hurt, surety. Certificate of Ruth herself.

THOMAS OVERSTREET and MARY CREASEY, November 10, 1795. Thomas Creasey, surety.

HENRY OLDAKERS and ELIZABETH TELLIS, December 27, 1794. Richard Tellis, surety. Consent of John Oldakers, father of Henry.

THOMAS OGLESBY and MARTHA BRADLEY, January 8, 1773. James Martin, surety. Consent of Wm. Bradley, father of Martha.

JONATHAN PRATHER and SARAH MOSELEY, September 30, 1780. James Mozley, surety. Consent of Edward Mozley, father of Sarah.

JAMES PENN and PEGGY COWAN, February 20, 1787. James Steptoe, surety. Consent of Robt. Cowan, father of Peggy.

THOMAS PALMER and ELIZABETH DAWSON, April 28, 1792. Julius Jones, surety. Consent of Abraham Dawson, father of Elizabeth.

EZEKIEL POTTS and ELANOR HARBISON, August 12, 1780. Robt. Russell, surety.

PETER PURNAL and ELIZABETH R. HUGHES, August 20, 1793. William Halley, surety. Consent of John Hughes, father of Elizabeth.

JOSEPH PREAST and SARAH EADS, November 15, 1799. Edward Eads, surety.

WILLIAM POWELL and USLEY HARDWICK, June 28, 1792. Jacob Wade, surety. Consent of Robert Hardwick, father of Usley.

REUBEN PITMAN and MARY ROBERTS, November 16, 1785. George Hughes, surety. Certificate of Mary herself.

HENRY PREAS and RACHEL JARRED, December 3, 1791. Thomas Preas, surety.

LEWIS PETIT and MARY CARR, August 13, 1787. Henry Mayberry, surety. Certificate of Mary herself.

THOMAS PHILIPS and MARY OWELL, April 9, 1789. John Allen, surety.

PETER PURNAL and PHEBE WOOD, February 15, 1792. Jeremiah Wood, surety. Consent of Thomas Wood, father of Phebe.

JOHN PATE and BETTY HAYNES, January 19, 1788. John Hampton, surety. Consent of Henry Haynes, father of Betty.

JAMES PRITCHARD and MARY MIDDLETON, May 22, 1784. Alexr. Gibbs, surety.

JOSEPH PENN and SALLY KING, April 20, 1790. Martin King, surety.

WILLIAM PADGET and ELIZABETH MERRITT, December 15, 1798. Thomas Merritt, surety.

JOHN PORTER and ANN AKIN, October 13, 1773. Alexander Dobbins, surety. Certificate of Ann herself.

JAMES PHELPS and RUTH GRANT, January 15, 1794. Richard Thurman, surety. Consent of John Grant, father of Ruth.

WILLIAM PERKINS and KISIAH ESTES, November 23, 1792. Roger Williams, surety. Certificate of Kisier herself that she is of full age.

JAMES PRITCHARD and MARY AIRL, August 5, 1779. Wm. Moon, Jacob Moon, Jr., and Zach. Gilliam, sureties. Certificate of Mary herself.

THOMAS PETIT and JUDITH ROYER, October 22, 1787. Joseph Hardy, surety. Certificate of Judith herself.

REUBEN PRICKETT and ELIZABETH DAY, January 4, 1773. Matthew Talbot, surety.

SAMUEL POINDEXTER and ANNE POINDEXTER SLAUGHTER, June 11, 1790. Joseph Poindexter, surety.

THOMAS PAGE and BETSEY ANN BELLAMY, December 5, 1796. Samuel Bellamy, surety.

JOHN PATRICK and ELIZABETH CALLAWAY, November 26, 1787. James Kerr, surety. Consent of Wm. Callaway.

HATTEN PRICE and JOICE CUNDIFF, February 26, 1787. Isaac Berry, surety. Consent of Thomas Price, father of Hatten; and of Mary Cundiff, the mother of Joice.

THOMAS POLLARD and CHIZIA (or OHIZIA) HUNT, August 1, 1778. Crispin Hunt, surety.

STEPHEN PRATT and SALLEY DABNEY, July 25, 1791. John Overstreet, surety. Consent of Cornelius Dabney, father of Salley.

STEPHEN PERROW and ELIZABETH FLEMING, May 11, 1778. John Forbes, surety. Consent of David Fleming, father of Elizabeth.

ISAAC PRESTON and SALLY HURT, September 22, 1800. Elisha Hurt, surety.

JOHN PERRIN and NANCEY WITT, December 5, 1794. John Witt, surety.

THOMAS PRESTON and LYDDA PULLEN, March 7, 1800. Thomas Pullen, surety.
Consent of David Saunders, guardian of Lydda.

JAMES PRICE and POLLY BURRAS, February 5, 1800. John Pate, surety.
Consent of Polly Burruss and Edmund Burruss.

RICHARD PRICE and FRANCES HENDERSON, December 23, 1788. Wm. Henderson,
surety.

THOMAS PRICE and MARGARET McCOY, October 9, 1782. David Clay, surety.
Consent of Anna Stump and John Stump, mother and step-father
of Margaret.

BENJAMIN PARKS and VIRLINCHE BRANCH, March 28, 1774. Arthur Mosely,
surety. Consent of Oliver Branch, father of Virlinche.

RICHARD PHELPS and SARAH WOODCOCK, August 31, 1791. Charles Perrin,
surety. Consent of Henry and Nelley Woodcock, parents of Sarah.

THOMAS PULLEN and ELIZABETH ABSTON, January 26, 1789. Simmons Everett,
surety. Consent of Jesse Abston, father of Elizabeth.

JOHN PHELPS and SUSANNA YOUNGER, August 13, 1787. Jesse Grubb, surety.
Consent of Ann Younger, mother of Susanna.

PHILIP PANKEY and ANN BROWN, February 4, 1788. William Gibson, surety.
Consent of Gross Scruggs. (Does not show why he gave it.)

STEPHEN PRESTON and ELIZABETH PULLEN, December 8, 1792. John Preston,
surety. Consent of Thomas Pullen, father of Elizabeth.

GEORGE PHILLIPS, batchelor and MARY JENNINGS, widow, March 21, 1768. W.
Leftwich, surety.

WILLIAM PENN and POLLY FURBUSH, June 9, 1800. Thomas Stewart, surety.
Consent of Charles Statham, grandfather of Polly.

GABRIEL PENN and SARAH CALLAWAY, September 24, 1761. Richard Callaway,
surety.

JAMES PAGE and FRANCES REYNOLDS, March 13, 1797. William Stewart, surety.
Consent of William Page, father of James; also of Charles
Reynolds.

LITTLEBERRY PARISH and MARY GEDDY, December 27, 1779. Bartholomew Geddy,
surety. Consent of George Geddy, father of Mary.

JAMES PATTESON (widower) and MARTHA BOYD, April 24, 1770. Wm. Boyd,
surety.

JOHN PATTERSON and MARY DICKSON, October 7, 1799. George Dickson, surety.

JOEL PRESTON and LUCY TATE, November 7, 1796. Hinman Wooster, surety.
Consent of Nancy Tate.

SAMUEL PARSONS and BETSEY PATTERSON, January 8, 1793. William Patterson,
surety.

JOHN PATE and MARY ABSTON, October 12, 1792. Jesse Abston, surety.

STEPHEN PHILLIPS and NANCY JETER, October 3, 1787. Henry Jeter, surety.

JESSE PRESTON and MILLEY MITCHELL, November 19, 1798. Elijah Mitchell, surety.

PETER PELTER and NANCY CANDLER, October 12, 1795. Zedekiah Candler, surety.

STEPHEN PRESTON and ELIZABETH SMITH, July 30, 1781. Micajah Ballard, surety. Consent of Judith Smith, mother of Elizabeth.

BENJAMIN ALLEN PATE and JUDITH PATE, December 16, 1790. John Pate, surety. Consent of Jeremiah Pate.

JOHN POLLARD and CATHARINE NICHOLLS, January 6, 1787. Thomas Pollard, surety. Consent of John Nicholls.

ANDREW PATTERSON and LUCY SCOTT, May 21, 1793. William Scott, surety.

GEORGE POTTER and HANNAH FITZHUGH, June 11, 1782. Wm. Ewing, surety. Consent of Robt. Fitzhugh.

PLEDGE PARMORE and SALLY HANSFORD, December 3, 1781. Charles Stevens, surety. Consent of John Hansford, father of Sally.

JOHN PRATT AND POLLY HAIL, September 7, 1792. Stephen Pratt, surety.

JAMES PATTESON, batchelor, and ELIZABETH CARSON, December 2, 1763. James Carson, surety. Certificate of Elizabeth herself that she is of full age.

DUDLEY POOL and KATHRINE DONAWAY, May 17, 1790. Thomas Robertson, surety. Certificate of Kathrine herself.

BOURNE PRICE and CENA CALLAWAY, March 5, 1773. Robt. Alexander, surety. Consent of Wm. Callaway, father of Seney, dated March 5, 1774.

DAVID PAGAN and MARY HARMAN, September 28, 1793. Jesse Hix, surety.

GEORGE PARKER and FRANCES OAKS, May 1, 1797. Thomas Dixon, surety.

JARRET PATTERSON and JANE ERWIN, December 24, 1798. Jonas Erwin, surety.

DANIEL PRICE and LYDIA MORRIS, March 28, 1781. William Price, surety.

WILLIAM PARISH and PATTY GOODE, December 7, 1778. James DeWitt, surety. Certificate of Patty herself.

ROGER QUARLES and POLLEY TRIGG, September 24, 1792. William Trigg, Jr., surety. Consent of William Trigg.

JOHN QUINN and LYDDA BRAMBLETT, March 10, 1790. Robert Rowland, surety. Consent of Anna Bramblett, mother of Lydda.

MATTHIAS REYNOLDS and MARTHA GOODMAN, November 18, 1788. Chas. Reynolds, surety.

JOHN ROSSER and ELIZABETH STRANGE, February 28, 1780. James Wilson, surety. Consent of John Strange.

WILLIAM RICE and REBECKAH ELLINGTON, August 13, 1781. William Newsom, surety.

WILLIAM RUCKER, of Amherst County, and SALLY NORTH, March 2, 1782. Abraham North, surety.

GIDEON RUCKER and JOYCY READ, December 25, 1793. Thomas Rucker, surety. Consent of William Read, father of Joycy.

THOMAS RUCKER and SALLY READ, January 3, 1793. James Rucker, surety. Consent of William Read, father of Sally.

WHITEHEAD RYAN, JUNR., and MARY BALENGE WADE, December 15, 1778. Jesse Hilton, surety. Certificate filed with this bond, but I can't read it.

ALEXANDER REYNOLDS and JEMIMA BRIGHT, December 29, 1790. Charles Bright, Jr., surety. Consent of Charles Bright, Sr., father of Jemima.

BENJAMIN RICE and MARY HENRY, December 8, 1790. William Burton, surety.

NICHOLAS ROBINSON and ELIZABETH BAGBEY, October 6, 1794. James English, surety. Consent of William Bagbey, father of Elizabeth.

JOHN RICHARDSON and MARY WILLIAMSON, May 9, 1798. Stephen McPherson, surety. Consent of John Williamson, Sr.

JOHN RICHARDSON and NANCY MARTIN, February 18, 1793. Charles Cooper, surety. Consent of Thomas and Rachel Martin.

JEFFERY ROBERTSON and NANCY DICKERSON, January 9, 1792. George Dabney, surety. Consent of Joseph and Elizabeth Dickerson.

BENJAMIN RAMSEY and SARAH WILLIAMS, August 13, 1796. John Williams, Jr., surety. Consent of Barth. Ramsay, father of Benjamin; and consent of John Williams.

WILLIAM RICHARDSON and RACHEL MANN, January 26, 1795. Chas. Caffery Martin, surety. Consent of Rachel herself.

JOHN REESE and ANN BROWN, December 5, 1792. James Brown, surety. Certificate of Ann that she is of age.

Obediah Reynolds and POLLY PEATROSS, November 24, 1798. James Peatross, surety.

ROBERT ROSS and NANCY FRITH, December 22, 1788. John Ross, surety. Consent of Joseph Frith, father of Nancy.

FRANCIS READ and FLORENCE BLACKBURN, December 16, 1774. Alexander Blackburn, surety. Consent of Andrew Blackburn.

GEORGE RUSSELL, batchelor, and SARAH WITCHER, spinster, May ___, 1769. Thomas Harris, surety. Consent of John Witcher, father of Sarah.

JAMES RAY and MARY TALLY, May 2, 1785. Alexander Gibbs, surety.

GEORGE REID and RACHEL CARR, September 10, 1792. William McCalam, surety.

MOSES RENTFRO and ELIZABETH TURPIN, May 24, 1773. Robert Alexander, surety. Consent filed, but cannot make out the name.

JACOB REED and NANCEY THOMAS, April 17, 1800. Frederick Gooldey, surety. Consent of William Thomas, the father [sic] of Nancey.

CORNELIUS ROACH and ELIZABETH WADE, February 17, 1800. James Wade, surety. Consent of David Wade, father of Elizabeth, also of Fanny Wade, her mother.

BENJAMIN RICE and POLLEY WILSON, January 8, 1796. George Wilson, surety. Consent of Joseph Wilson.

BENJAMIN RAMSAY and BETTY BANNISTER, June 13, 1785. James Bannister, surety.

WILLIAM RHODES and ANN DEWITT, December 21, 1798. Aaron Dewitt, surety. Consent of Mary R. Dewitt, the mother of Ann.

LUKE RAY and SARAH WARNER, January 23, 1799. John W. Claytor, surety.

WILLIAM ROBERTSON and MARY FREEMAN, July 27, 1795. James Freeman, surety.

BENJAMIN RICHARDS and POLLY SMITH, November 27, 1797. Andrew Smith, surety. Consent of Alex. H. Smith, father of Polly.

JOHN REESE and MARY BOWYER, July 23, 1794. Lewis Speece, surety. Consent of Mary Boyer, Sen'r., mother of Mary.

JOHN ROSS and ELENOR MITCHELL, January 11, 1787. Geo. Bozwell, surety. Certificate of Elenor that she is of age.

FRANCIS READ and MARGARET BOYD, April 6, 1762. Alexander Boyle, surety.

ROBERT ROWLAND and TABY WHITE, August 9, 1790. Wm. Leftwich, Jr., surety. Consent of Stephen White, father of Taby.

JOSEPH ROY and FRANKEY PETIT, December ___, 1793. Thos. Pettit, surety. Certificate from Wm. Ewing, saying that the father of Frankey has no objections.

HENRY RUSHER and ELIZABETH THOMAS, January 23, 1786. Philip Boyd, surety. Certificate: "Sir, please to isue out licence of marrage between Henry Rusher & Elizabeth Thomas, This is to certify the young woman is under a good carrecter among her neighbours. Witness our hands, John Phillip Weaver, Cathron Weaver, George Rusher."

DAVID ROGERS and MARY CHRISTIAN, May 18, 1762. Wm. Bumpass, surety.

NATHANIEL REYNOLDS and ELIZABETH ANN BOWYER, May 1, 1795. Adam Bowyer, surety.

JOHN RICE and FANNY SNELSON, October 8, 1792. Stephen Hubbard, surety. Consent of Charles Snelson, father of Fanny.

JESSE ROBERTSON and MARY O'BRIAN, September 9, 1793. Thomas Robertson, surety. Consent of Mathew O'Brian, father of Mary.

JOSEPH ROSS and PATTY CHILDRESS, June 30, 1789. Richard Davis, surety. Consent of Elizabeth Childress, mother of Patty.

ARTHUR ROBERTSON and BETSEY IRVINE, January 4, 1781. Robert Bradfute, surety.

BENJAMIN ROBERTSON and SUSANNA NORTH, March 24, 1783. Abram North, surety.

THOMAS RICHARDS and BARBARA RAMSEY, November 25, 1771. Isham Talbot, surety.

FIELD ROBINSON and MARY ARTHUR, March 25, 1773. Gross Scruggs, surety.

THOMAS ROBERTSON and ELIZABETH CANDLER, February 8, 1790. John Taylor, surety. Consent of Zebedee Candler, father of Elizabeth.

JOSHUA RICHARDSON and MARY SNOW, January 12, 1788. Anderson Milton, surety. Consent of Thos. Arthur, Sen'r., for Mary Snow, his step-daughter.

JAMES REID and FANNY WILLSON, September 24, 1798. Henry Eidson, surety. Consent of James Willson, father of Fanny.

CHARLES READY and SALLY MASON, August 4, 1794. William Frith, surety. Consent of Mary Dale, for her son Charles Ready. Consent of Elizabeth Keenum, for her daughter Sally Mason.

NATHANIEL ROUNDTREE and ELIZABETH WORLEY, February 24, 1783. Matthew Worley, surety. Consent of William Worley, father of Elizabeth.

LEONARD ROBERTS and NANCY RILEY, August 23, 1785. Domnick Walch, surety. Certificate of Nancy herself.

DAVID RICE and JANE HOLT, June 16, 1794. Mary Rice, surety. Consent of Betty Holt, mother of Jane.

WILLIAM ROBINSON and MASON GIBBS, September 19, 1791. Alexr. Gibbs, surety.

JAMES RUSSELL and ROSANNA RUTHERFORD, February 14, 1778. Robert Russell, surety. Consent of William Rutherford, father of Rosanna.

JOHN REYNOLDS and NANCEY MILLAM, March 14, 1800. Jesse Bradley, surety. Consent of Zachariah Millam, the father of Nancey.

REUBEN RAGLAND and ELIZABETH CLIBOURN, December 17, 1795. Geo. Medley, surety.

JONATHAN ROSSER, widower, and NANCY HELM, widow, January 23, 1782. Jesse Wood, surety. Certificate of Nancy.

WILLIAM RUSHER and ELIZABETH BRICKY, January 9, 1792. George Rusher, surety. Certificate of Elizabeth herself.

WILLIAM RICHARDSON and POLLY FINNEY, September 15, 1796. John Finney, surety. Consent of Peter Finney, the father of Polly.

JOSEPH RIDGEWAY and ESTHER NICHOLS, August 14, 1784. William Nichols, surety. Consent of Bazdell Nichols, the father of Esther.

JAMES ROBINSON and SARAH ROBINSON, October 9, 1772. John Robinson, surety. Certificate of Sarah herself. John Robinson swears that she is 21 years old.

THOMAS RATLIFFE and MARY BROWN, October 22, 1779. Alexander Dobbins, surety. Certificate of Mary herself.

WILLIAM RICE and ALLEY GOODRICH, May 14, 1796. Thomas Goodrich, surety. Consent of James Goodrich and Charles Rice, Senr.

JOHN ROUTON and JANE ARTHUR, November 22, 1779. Benj. Galloway, surety. Consent of Martha Arthur, mother of Jane.

CHARLES REYNOLDS and NANCEY PALMER, December 18, 1799. Jesse Lockett, surety. Consent of Benjamin Palmore, the father of Nancey.

GEORGE ROBINS and JINNEY SMITH, October 30, 1799. Sam Smith, surety.

JAMES RUCKER and NANCY READ, January 31, 1788. Edmund Tate, surety. Consent of William Read, father of Nancy.

THOMAS ROWLAND, batchelor, and MARY RUSSELL, spinster, June 6, 1768. Stephen Goggin, surety.

MICAJAH ROLAND and SIDNEY EWING, October 12, 1793. John Ewing, surety. Consent of John Ewing, father of Sidney.

REUBEN ROWLAND and PATSEY EWING, August 20, 1792. William Ewing, surety.

WILLIAM RAY and HOPE SUTTON, January 6, 1796. Benjamin Ray, surety. Consent of Chris'r. Sutton, father of Hope.

GEORGE RICHARDSON and MOLLEY THURMAN, August 25, 1794. John Thurman, surety.

NATHANIEL REEVES and MIRIAM ERWIN, October 26, 1795. Joseph Erwin, surety.

BARNETT RICHARDSON and ELIZABETH MARTIN, April 13, 1789. Finch Criddle, surety. Consent of Thomas Martin, father of Elizabeth.

JOHN ROACH and AMY JARREL, July 8, 1786. Henry Roach, surety. Consent of David Jarrel, father of Amy.

JAMES RUCKER and EUPHAN TATE, May 30, 1781. Caleb Tate, surety. Consent of Henry Tate, father of Euphan.

GEORGE RAY and MARY WEBSTER, September 1, 1779. John Webster, surety. Consent of Richard Webster, father of Mary; and of Mary Ray, mother of George.

JAMES RICHARDSON and MARGARET CALDWELL, August 29, 1780. John Richardson, surety. Consent of Geo. Caldwell "This is to inform you the match is broak off between my Daughter Margaret and Daniel White, please to grant James Richardson a license. I am Sir, your Humbl. Servt. Geo. Caldwell".

JOHN STAPLES and MARTHA STOVALL, January 13, 1778. Oren Franklin, surety. Consent of George Stovall, Jr., father of Martha.

JOHN STONE and ELIZABETH STOVALL, December 22, 1782. Augustine Leftwich, Sr., surety.

WILLIAM STONE and NANCY DOOLEY, August 10, 1791. Thomas Dooley, surety.

JOHN SALMON and ELIZABETH OWELL, January 31, 1787. John Allen, surety.

WILLIAM SOUTH and KATY DANIEL, October 8, 1785. John Daniel, surety.

JOHN SHELTON and ANNE POINDEXTER, March 13, 1786. Joseph Poindexter, surety.

ALEXANDER SINCLAIR and REBECKAH GILPIN, November 25, 1799. Francis G. Gilpin, surety.

THOMAS SNOW and RACHEL BENNETT, October 10, 1781. John Adams, Jr., surety.

JOHN SLATON and ELIZABETH HIBBS, November 28, 1791. James Bunch, surety.

LEVI SILVERS and KITTY READY, April 25, 1791. William Buford, Jr., surety.

JOHN STONE and ELIZABETH DOOLEY, August 3, 1796. John Dooley, surety.

ARCHA STRATTON and EDNEY DICKERSON, October 10, 1793. Joseph Dickerson, surety.

BENJAMIN SINOR and POLLY MERIDY, January 23, 1797. John Hackney, surety.

ABRAHAM SLACK and MARY HUDDLESTON, November 7, 1798. Henry Loyd, surety.

THOMAS SNYDER and NANCY DOVE, December 28, 1797. Bingham Mays, surety.

ISAAC SINCLAIR and FRANCES CARTER, May 7, 1800. Merry Carter, surety.

LEWIS SPEECE and SARAH PAGEN, August 26, 1796. David Pagen, surety.

GROSS SCRUGGS, batchelor and ELIZABETH ARTHUR, spinster, October 4, 1768.
    Isham Talbot, surety.

GEORGE STANDLEY and MARY CREWS, October 24, 1791. Jesse Crews, surety.

NATHANIEL SHREWSBURY and ELIZABETH McGEORGE, November 26, 1798. Benj.
    Stith, surety.

REUBEN SIMMONS and EPSEY PATTERSON, November 7, 1795. William Patterson,
    surety.

JAMES STANTON and MARY HOLLOWAY, August 18, 1792. Isaac Holloway, surety.

GEORGE STEEL and SALLY GILLIAM, December 21, 1789. Richard Gilliam,
    surety.

JOHN SHARPE, batchelor, and ANNE DOOLEY, spinster, January 25, 1762.
    James Boyd and Gross Scruggs, sureties.

JAMES SHANNON and MARY REID, August 9, 1797. Samuel Reid, surety.

WILLIAM SHREWSBURY and RHODA PATE, December 23, 1799. Ruel Shrewsbury,
    surety.

FRANCIS STEEL and ELIZABETH NEAL, June 28, 1784. George Asbury, surety.

BEN SCOTT and TEMPE DAY (alias RUFF) November 3, 1792. John Urquhart,
    surety.

THOMAS SCRUGGS and JUDITH BUFORD, February 27, 1787. James Buford,
    surety.

ABRAHAM SHARP and ANNE REID, December 12, 1789. Paulser Smelser, surety.

WILLIAM STEWART and NANCY DOOLEY, April 26, 1784. Thomas Dooley, Jr.,
    surety.

HENRY SMITH, batchelor, and MARY BIRKS, spinster, May 26, 1761. John
    Partree Birks, surety.

PAUL TAULBOTT SUMMERS and SARAH BRUCE, May 26, 1789. Mordecai Bruce
    (Howard), surety.

JOHN STEVENS and SUSANNAH SPEECE, July 3, 1781. Conrad Speece, surety.

THOMAS SMITH and BETSEY HAYNES, February 25, 1788. Henry Haynes,
    surety.

JEREMIAH SWAIN and ELIZABETH WATTS, December 19, 1798. Charles Swain and Benj. Watts, sureties.

ROBERT SCARBOROUGH and MARY McGUIRE, November 28, 1785. Lawrence McGuire, surety.

JOHN STRATTON and MARY ANN TURNER, January 29, 1788. Admire Turner, surety.

JAMES R. SANDERS and MARGOTT REID, October 10, 1798. Francis Reid, surety.

ROBERT STRANGE, of Campbell County, and ELIZABETH EARLY, July 16, 1791. Joshua Early, surety.

JAMES STEPTOE and FANNY CALLAWAY, February 14, 1781. Robert Alexander, surety.

JOHN SMITH and PEGGY CRUMPTON, December 19, 1800. David Crumpton, surety.

FREDERICK WILLIAM SHUNK and SARAH PARRISH, spinster, May 28, 1767. Alexander Parrish, surety.

REUBEN SIMMONS and FRANCES GLASS, July 23, 1779. Benjamin Tanner, surety. Consent of Vincent Glass, father of Frances.

WILLIAM HARRISON SANDERS and WINFRED HANCOCK, February 28, 1791. Samuel Hancock, surety. Consent of William Hancock, father of Winfred.

WILLIAM SPRADLIN and BATHSHEBA HOLLAND, December 2, 1786. Wm. Ball, surety. Consent of Bershaba, that she is of age.

VALENTINE STURMAN and MARGARET IRVINE, March 16, 1778. Samuel Claytor, surety. Request of Margaret herself.

NEWBURY STOCKTON and BETHSHABAH BRANON, January 10, 1801. Jesse Hix and Edward Greene, sureties. Consent of Laurence Branon, father of Bethshabah.

JOHN SMITH and SUSANNA SCARBOROUGH, March 22, 1787. William Thornhill, surety. Consent of Robert Scarborough, father of Susanna.

THOMAS STUART and POLLY WHEAT, July 16, 1799. Israel Winfrey, surety. Consent of Joseph Wheat, father of Polly.

AUGUSTINE SMITH and SARAH HALL, February 26, 1800. John Smith, surety. Consent of Hezekiah, father of Sarah.

JOHN SHACKLEFORD and PENELOPE ADAMS, August 15, 1778. James Shackleford, surety. Consent of Robert Adams, the father of Penelope.

JOHN SCOTT and LUCY BUNDURANT, September 10, 1795. Littleberry Bundurant, surety. Consent of Joel Bondurant.

THOMAS SCOTT and ANNE COOKSEY, October 2, 1790. Lamester Cooksey, surety. Consent of Anne herself.

WILLIAM SHEPHERD and ESTHER WHIRLEY, January 10, 1780. William Hatton, surety. Consent of William Whirley, father of Esther.

THOMAS STRATTON and ELIZABETH LEFTWICH, December 2, 1795. James Leftwich, surety. Consent of Thomas Leftwich, the father of Betsy.

WILLIAM SCRUGGS and BETTY BUFORD, January 29, 1784. James Steptoe, surety. Consent of James Buford, father of Betty.

CAIN SCANTLING and SARAH PHILIPS, November 5, 1787. Nathaniel Shrewsbury, surety. Consent of Samuel Philips, father of Sarah.

WILLIAM SCOTT and PRISCILLA BUNCH, January 31, 1792. Baxton Gentry, surety. Consent of James Bunch, father of Priscilla.

COLEMAN SMITH and TABITHA HATCHER, March 25, 1793. Samuel Hatcher, surety. Consent of Benjamin Hatcher.

HENDRICK SUTPHIN and RACHEL OWEN, December 17, 1788. William Sutphin, surety. Consent of Owen Owen and Mary Owen, parents of Rachel.

SAMSON SHARP and NANCY DOOLEY, March 4, 1790. Noah Sharp, surety. Consent of George Dooley, Senr., father of Nancy.

WILLIAM SCOTT and MARY THACKSTON, March 6, 1792. Peter Scott, surety. Consent of John and Elizabeth Baker "which are all the parents she have alive".

THOMAS SMITH and ANNA WADE, September 11, 1798. James Wade, surety. Consent of Anna herself.

JOEL SALMON and EVEY KELLEY, November 22, 1790. Samuel Hatcher, surety. Consent of Nancy Kelley, mother of Evey.

JAMES SPENCE and ELENOR MILAN, October 1, 1785. Congrave Jackson, surety. Consent of Ann Milan, mother of Elenor.

DRURY SCOTT and FRANKEY AMPEY, January 14, 1794. Benjamin Scott, surety. Certificate of William Ewing, saying they are Mulattoes.

WILLIAM SAUNDERS and HOLLY CURLE, June 16, 1798. Robert Adams, surety. Consent of Jus. (Jno.) Curle, brother of Holly.

JONATHAN SMITH and ELIZABETH WOOD, March 14, 1791. James Wood, surety. Consent of Thomas Wood, father of Elizabeth.

THOMAS SMITH and CUZZY BUNDRANT, October 1, 1785. William Harris, surety. Consent of John Bundrant.

ALEXANDER SIMMONS and ONEY PATTERSON, February 24, 1794. Wayman Sinclair, surety. Consent of William Patterson, father of Oney.

CHARLES SMITH and ELIZABETH HOWERTON, August 4, 1786. John Owen, surety. Consent of Lucy Howerton, mother of Elizabeth.

PLEASANT STANDLEY and DELPHIA HUNTER, November 3, 1789. John Goff, surety. Consent of Peter Hunter.

JOHN SHERLEY and ELIZABETH SHIELS, November 16, 1791. John Golloway, surety. Consent of Elenor Shiels, mother of Elizabeth.

JOHN STAPLES and JUDITH COBBS, December 26, _____(James Wood, Gov.). Consent of Edmund Cobbs, father of Judith. William Cobbs, surety.

THOMAS STERLING and ELIZABETH CAMPBELL, January 10, 1792. James Board, surety. Consent of Elizabeth herself, saying that she is of age.

STEPHEN SMELSER and TABBY BROWN, January 17, 1794. Archibald Lamb, surety. Consent of James Brown, father of Tabby.

HARRIS STANDLEY and RACHEL MARTIN, September 28, 1787. Joseph Martin, surety. Consent of Job Martin and Elizabeth Martin, parents of Rachel.

GEORGE SWAIN and PATTY HUTSON, February 27, 1786. Robert Hutson, surety. Consent of Joel Hutson, father of Patty.

EDWARD SPRADLING and LUCY BROWN, June 14, 1791. Joseph Wright, surety. Consent of John and Mary Brown, parents of Lucie.

REUBEN STANDLY and ESTHER PATTERSON, January 15, 1791. Jonas Jordan, surety. Consent of Joseph Patterson, father of Esther.

JAMES STEVENS and MARTHA MORRIS, July 24, 1780. John Morris, surety. Consent of Samuel Morris.

ABNER SPRADLIN and SARAH ADKERSON, September 6, 1790. Benj. Meador, surety. Consent of John Adkerson, father of Sarah.

WILLIAM SHOEMAKER and JANE OVERSTREET, January 13, 1796. Chas. Overstreet, surety. Consent of James Overstreet, the father of Jane.

WILLIAM SELF and DICEY VAUGHAN, January 21, 1796. Joseph Barrington, surety. Consent of William Vaughan, the father of Dicey.

DABNEY SHREWSBURY and ELIZABETH SINCLAIR, October 9, 1786. John Shrewsbury, surety. Consent of Isaac Sinclair, father of Elizabeth.

ISAAC SERNONES and MARY MIKLE, March 16, 1796. William Sernones, surety. Consent of Mary herself.

ISAAC SINKLER and ANNA KERNS, July 25, 1796. Thomas Preas, surety. Consent of Annar Carnes herself.

MATTHIAS SLACK and SARAH LOYD, May 14, 1796. Levi Squires, surety. Consent of Henry Loyd, father of Sarah.

NOAH SHARP and JENNY DOOLEY, December 10, 1792. George Dooley, surety. Consent of George Dooley, father of Jeney.

THOMAS STUMP and MARY HORE, September 23, 1793. John Nichols, surety. Consent of Edward Hore, father of Mary.

WILLIAM STRATTON and MARY HAYNES, November 30, 1793. Archibald Stratton, surety. Consent of Mary saying she is of full age.

RICHARD SHAON and ANN KASEY, September 24, 1792. David Shaon, surety. Consent of James Kasey, father of Ann.

DAVID SINKLER and LUCY BURTON, December 10, 1799. Isaac Sinkler, surety. Consent of Jacob Burton, father of Lucy.

NATHAN SOLMONS and SALLY TAYLOR, June 9, 1798. Joshua Taylor, surety. Consent of Richard Taylor.

BENJAMIN SAMPSON and JUDAH PERRIN, October 3, 1792. Charles Perrin, surety. Consent of John Perrin, father of Judah.

ANDREW STEEL and JANE ASBERRY, February 8, 1794. Francis Steel, surety. Consent of Thomas and Martha Asbury.

ADMIRE STONE and SUSANNA GILPIN, April 11, 1794. William Stone, surety. Certificate of Susanna that she is of full age.

JOHN SHANNON and JENE REID, October 22, 1792. Alex. Reid, surety. Consent of Jas. Reid, father of Jene.

JEREMIAH SCANTLIN and TABBY DOSS, September 27, 1794. Morgin Morgin, surety. Consent of Hinman Wooften and Tibet Wooften (Woofter).

DAVID SAUNDERS and LOCKEY LEFTWICH, August 30, 1788. Joseph Holt, surety. Consent of Augustine Leftwich, father of Lockey.

NATHANIEL SHREWSBURY and NANCY BOARD, March 12, 1792. William Board, surety. Consent of James Board, father of Nancy.

JOHN SINKLER and BETSEY PATTERSON, February 20, 1798. Alexander Simmons, surety. Consent of William Patterson, uncle of Betsy.

ABRAHAM SMELSER and SALLY SMITH, April 25, 1791. Archibald Lamb, surety. Consent of Samuel Greenwood, uncle of Sally.

THOMAS SQUIRES and JEMIMA BOARD, January 27, 1800. James Cundiff, surety. Consent of John Board, father of Jemima.

RUEL SHREWSBURY and SARAH SINKLER, December 19, 1788. Nathl. Shrewsbury, surety. Consent of Isaac Sinkler, father of Sarah.

JACOB STIFF and RHODA SCOTT, March 27, 1787. James Stiff, surety. Consent of Rody, herself.

JOHN SLED and MILLEY HENSLEY, July 9, 1791. James Hensley, surety. Consent of Lillay (or Sillay) Hensley.

GROSS SCRUGGS and NANCY LOGWOOD, May 28, 1792. William Buford, surety. Consent of Thomas Logwood, the father of Nancy.

ZACHARIAH SUMERS and SARAH DAWSON, March 1, 1786. Peter Fitzhugh, surety. Consent of John Dawson and Susannah Dawson, parents of Sarah. Also consent of Rachil Sumers, mother of Zachariah.

THOMAS SALE and SALLY HARDWICK, March 28, 1791. John Hardwick, surety.

WILLIAM P. SKILLERN and HANNAH BRAXTON BROOKE, December 16, 1799. Callohill Mennis, surety.

JOHN SINCLAIR (SINKLER) and JUDAH BURTON, July 23, 1798. Thomas Scott, surety.

EDWARD SINCLAIR and JOANNAH HUDNALL, January 11, 1799. Jeremiah Hilton, surety.

LEVIE SQUIRES and MARY CUNDIFF, March 13, 1778. William Hancock, surety.

SAMUEL SMITH and MARTHA HATCHER, January 23, 1797. Thomas Smith, surety.

GEORGE SCOTT and DOSHIA DENT, February 17, 1799. John Dent, surety.

CHRISTOPHER SUTTON and NANCY MILAM, December 18, 1795. Caleb Tate, Jr., surety.

RICE SMITH and PEGGY ADAMS, June 5, 1781. Charles Lynch, Jr., surety.

WILLIAM SIMPSON and ELIZABETH READ, November 23, 1779. William Carson, surety. Consent of John Carson, saying he is nearest kin of Elizabeth.

JESSE STIFF and AMEY WILLIAMS, October 9, 1786. Thomas Williams, surety. Consent of John Stiff, father of Jesse.

WILLIAM SNIDER and BETSEY DEAREN, March 4, 1794. Abraham Morgan, surety. Consent of John Dearen, father of Betsey.

ROBERT STEVENS and MARGARET SHARTEL, July 7, 1781. Arches. Moon, surety. Consent of Jacob Shartel, father of Margaret.

CAUSBY SCOTT and SALLY STANDLEY, December 3, 1789. James Harris, surety. Consent of Sally herself, saying she is of full age.

ISAAC SMITH and MOURNING DAVENPORT, October 13, 1795. Joel Davenport, surety. Consent of Mary Davenport, mother of Mourning.

STEPHEN SANDERS, batchelor, and MILLY HAYNES, spinster, September 29, 1768. William Haynes, surety. Consent of William Haynes, father of Milly.

JOHN STRANGE and JANE BEAVER, December 25, 1780. John Lane, surety. Consent of Jane herself.

ROBERT SINCLAIR, JUNR. and LUCY PATTERSON, January 6, 1800. William Patterson, surety. Consent of Peter Patterson, Guardian of Lucy, who is orphan of Edward Patterson.

JOHN SISSON and JUDITH JOHNSON, November 22, 1799. William Timberlake, surety. Consent of Judith herself.

ABRAHAM SHARP and REBECCA ARMSTRONG, March 22, 1779. John Sharp, surety. Consent of William Armstrong, father of Rebecca.

CHRISTOPHER SCAGGS and TABITHA MORRIS, December 16, 1790. William Morris, surety. Consent of Elizabeth Morris, mother of Tabitha.

STEPHEN SMITH and ELIZABETH SMITH, November 8, 1778. Robert Alexander, surety. Consent of Guy Smith, father of Elizabeth.

JOHN SLACK and NANCEY HUDDLESTON, November 26, 1798. Thomas Alexander, surety. Consent of Mary Huddleston, mother of Nancey.

DANIEL TRIGG and ANN SMITH, January 30, 1777. Robert Alexander, surety. Consent of Guy Smith, father of Ann.

JOHN TRIGG, batchelor, and DIANNA AYRES, spinster, December 17, 1770. Barnard Gaines.

THOMAS THOMSON and KEZIAH ADAMS, May 28, 1781. Thos. Fuqua, surety.

JAMES THOMAS and CHLOE HOLLY, June 28, 1779. Francis Holly, surety.

EDWARD TILMAN and MOLLY JOHNSTON, October 29, 1781. Benjamin Johnston, surety.

WILLIAM TRACY and SARAH STEWARD, _____ 26, 1787. Charles Harris, surety.

THOMAS THORP and ELEANOR JACKSON, April 14, 1791. Jarvis Jackson, surety.

ADMIRE TURNER, JR. and LUCY HATCHER, December 18, 1800. Lewis Arthur, surety.

JOSHUA THOMAS and BETSY EWIN (ERWIN), August 27, 1795. Jonas Erwin, surety.

WILLIAM TAYLOR and LUCINDA GRIFFIN, December 22, 1800. William Campbell, surety.

JAMES THOMASON and NANCY HIX, April 25, 1796. Philips Hix, surety.

NATHANIEL TATE and SUSANNA GILLIAM, January 26, 1778. Archs. Moon, surety.

WILLIAM TOMPKINS and ELIZABETH COBB, June 25, 1781. Edmund Cobbs, surety.

RICHARD THURMAN and ELIZABETH RYNOR, November 24, 1794. George Rynor, surety.

GEORGE THOMAS and WINNEY ADAMS, November 27, 1797. Thomas Adams, surety.

FRANCIS THORP, batchelor, and ELIZABETH CALLAWAY, spinster, December 26, 1762. James Callaway, surety.

STEPHEN TRIGG and ELIZABETH CLARK, January 25, 1790. John Campbell, surety.

JOHN TAMPLIN (TEMPLAIN) and AGNESS WILLS, February 6, 1779. Jacob Eckols, surety.

BAZE THURMAN and MARGET OSBOURNE, November 20, 1791. John Osburne, surety.

ISHAM TALBOT, batchelor, and ELIZABETH DAVIS, spinster, April 29, 1765. Gross Scruggs, surety.

WILSON TURNER and ELIZABETH DOSS, April 12, 1796. Azariah Doss, surety.

JOHN THOMPSON and LYDIA QUINN, October 9, 1800. Charles Price, surety.

JOHN TAYLOR and SARAH ROBERTSON, February 23, 1789. Thomas Robertson, surety.

JOSIAH TURNER of Henry County and MILLEY KEY, November 26, 1783. George Key, surety.

JESSE TATE, batchelor, and MARGARET MILLER, spinster, August 27, 1771. James Callaway, surety.

THOMAS TUCKER and REBECCAH UPDIKE, October 28, 1799. Amon Updike, surety.

NATHANIEL TATE and RHODA TERRY, February 22, 1773. Stephen Goggin, surety.

WILLIAM TAYLOR and KATY READY, October 27, 1800. William Rose, surety.

JOHN TULEY, JUNR., of Amherst County, and MARY WILLIAMS, May 26, 1791. John Dawson, surety. Consent of Mary Williams.

WILLIAM THORP and ELVIRA PRICE, August 24, 1798. Samuel Holt, surety. Consent of Robert Price, father of Elvira.

PLUMMER THURSTON and MARY TALBOT, June 5, 1777. John Holt, surety. Consent of Charles Talbot, father of Mary.

WILLIAM F. TABLE and FRANCES GRANWOOD, May 15, 1797. Peter Follis, surety. Consent of Samuel Granwood, father of Frances.

ROBERT TRUEMAN and MARY KENNETT, December 24, 1798. Zachariah Kennett, surety. Consent of John and Katy Kinnet.

ALASON TRIGG and LUCY QUARLES, July 20, 1796. William Trigg, surety. Consent of Sarah Quarles.

JAMES TURNER and SALLY LEFTWICH, August 24, 1778. Robert Alexander, surety. Certificate of Jno. W. Holt, saying that Majr. Leftwich has given his consent to the marriage of his daughter Sally.

MATTHEW THOMPSON and NANCEY MANN, May 11, 1787. David Blankenship, surety. Consent of Charles Mann, father of Nancy.

BENJAMIN TURNER and ELIZABETH SHREWSBURY, November 8, 1791. James Cundiff, surety. Consent of Elizabeth Shrewsbury, mother of said Elizabeth.

WILLISTON TALBOT, batchelor, and ELIZABETH COCK, spinster, December 9, 1769. Isham Talbot, surety. Consent of George Cock, father of Elizabeth.

STOCKLEY TURNER and PATSEY HOLT, September 25, 1799. Joseph Holt, surety. Consent of Lucy Holt, mother of Patsey.

CHARLES TONEY and NANCEY READY, July 28, 1794. Charles Ready, surety. Consent of Richard and Mary Dale.

DAVID THORP and JANE CREWS, July 28, 1789. John Halley, surety. Consent of Jons. Crews and Jane Crews, parents of Jane.

JOHN TALBOT, batchelor, and SARAH ANTHONY, spinster, February 2, 1760. Gross Scruggs, surety. Consent of John Anthony, father of Sarah.

RICHARD TIMBERLAKE and SARAH DOUGHERTY, February 20, 1775. Charles Moorman, surety. Consent of Sarah herself.

RICHARD TURNER and RACHEL AYRES, December 11, 1792. Drury Holland, surety. Consent of James Ayres.

RICHARD TAYLOR and LUCY HYLTON, March 12, 1798. Isaac Wade, surety. Consent of Lucy herself.

WASHINGTON TAYLOR and ELVIRA NANCE, November 15, 1800. Allsup Taylor, surety. Consent of Elvira saying she is of full age.

WILLIAM TIMBERLAKE and MOURNING JOHNSON, February 19, 1798. Christopher Johnson, surety. Consent of Mourning saying she is 22 years of age.

HAIDEN TRIGG and MARTHA GATEWOOD, August 12, 1783. Robert Davis, surety. Consent of William Trigg, father of Hayden; also consent of James Gatewood, father of Martha.

OBADIAH TATE and NANCY GOGGIN, December 12, 1798. Samuel Clemens, surety. Consent of Rachel Goggin, mother of Nancy.

JOHN THOMAS and QUINTILLY PULLEN, February 4, 1793. John Carter, surety. Consent of Quintilly herself.

ARCHIBALD THOMAS and MARY HILL, April 13, 1791. Isaac Thomas, surety. Consent of Martha Hill, mother of Mary.

ISAAC THOMAS and MARY DEWITT, May 8, 1787. John Hill, surety. Consent
of John Ross Dewitt, father of Mary.

HENRY THURMAN and SARAH TERRELL, January 15, 1795. Joseph Thurman, surety.
Consent of Edward Terrel.

JAMES TURLEY and MARY SHAW, June 8, 1779. Samuel Fair, surety. Consent
of Mary herself.

MACKLON TISON (TYSON) and ELIZABETH EADS, December 3, 1792. William
Huddleston, surety. Consent of Robert Eads, the father of
Elizabeth.

JOHN TUNSTALL and FRANCES MARTIN, March 16, 1791. Thomas Martin, surety.
Consent of Frances herself.

HAILE TALBOT and ELIZABETH IRVINE, September 18, 1778. James Adams,
surety. Consent of David Irvine, father of Betsey.

FRANCIS THORPE, of Campbell County, and ELIZABETH SCRUGGS, November 13th,
1788. William Quarles, surety. Consent of Elizabeth herself.

JOHN THORP and RUTH RENNOLS, October 15, 1791. David Thorp, surety.
Consent of Charles Renols, father of Ruth.

WILLIAM TURNER and BETSEY HIX, January 23, 1788. William Hix, surety.
Consent of John Hix, father of Betsey.

EZEKIEL THORNHILL and NANCEY BARRETT, March 16, 1789. Isham Galloway,
surety. Consent of George and Sarah Barret, parents of Nancey.

WILLIAM TERRY and JENNY SMITH, June 26, 1781. Robert Alexander, surety.
Consent of Anne Smith, mother of Jenny.

THOMAS TOLLEY and LUCY JONES, July 31, 1798. James Kay, surety. Consent
of Nicolis and Susanna Jones, parents of Lucy.

WILLIAM THORNHILL and SUSANNA BARTON, February 25, 1789. Leonard Thornhill,
surety. Consent of Bur Barten, the father of Susanna.

GEORGE TULEY and PATSEY DAWSON, April 23, 1792. Charles Sparks, surety.
Consent of John and Susanna Dawson, parents of Patsey.

JOSEPH TOLLEY and POLLY WITTETO, November 18, 1785. John Rowse, surety.
Consent of Mary Witto, mother of Polly.

ENOCH TERRY and PEGGY HATCHER, December 25, 1797. Jeremiah Hatcher,
surety. Consent of Henry and Ann Hatcher, parents of Peggy.

CHRISTOPHER TOLLEY and PRISCILLA HILL, March 17, 1794. James Kay, surety.
Consent of Arther and Martha Markham, the stepfather and mother
of Priscilla.

JOSEPH THURMAN and NANCEY FRANKLIN, December 15, 1792. John Porter, surety.
Consent of Mary Ann Franklin, mother of Nancey.

THOMAS TERRY and POLLY MILAM, February 24, 1789. James White, surety.
Consent of Ann Milam, mother of Polly.

CHARLES THOMAS and ANN CRAIG, December 17, 1800. Samuel McCluer, surety.
Consent of Elizabeth Craige, the mother of Ann; also consent
of William Craige, the fater of Ann.

SOLOMAN TRACEY and KITTY MILLER McCARGO, August 25, 1783. David Douglass,
surety. Consent of Hugh McCargo, the father of Kitty.

CHARLES TONEY and ZELPAH BUNDURANT, December 19, 1796. Thomas Pollard,
surety. Consent of Zilphah saying that she is of full age.

SAMUEL UPDIKE and JEMIMA WILLICE, April 24, 1799. George Willis, surety.

JACOB UHL and POLLY BEST, October 13, 1787. Samuel Best, surety. Consent
of John Best, father of Polly.

FREDERICK UHL and PHEEBY PRICE, November 26, 1792. John Ayres, surety.
Consent of Pheeby herself.

BENJAMIN VAUGHAN and SUSANNA BURNETT, May 13, 1795. Elisha Burnett,
surety.

HENRY VANOVER and NANCY GOIN, August 28, 1795. Isham Goin and Jeremiah
Goin, sureties. Consent of William Goin, father of Nancy.

WILLIAM VARNUM and MARY O'NEAL, November 7, 1786. John Steel, surety.
Consent of Daniel O'Neal, father of Mary, and of Elizabeth
Varmun, mother of William.

JOSEPH VEAL, of Amherst County, and Elizabeth King, May 10, 1797. Martin
King, surety. Consent of Martha King, mother of Elizabeth, and
of William Veal, father of Joseph.

JOHN VAUGHAN and MARY ARTER, December 13, 1797. Daniel Laughorn, surety.
Consent of Mary Arter.

EDWARD VEST and STELLEY CHEEK, July 15, 1794. John Creasey, surety.
Consent of Will Cheek, father of Stelley.

OBEDIAH VAUGHN and ELIZABETH EDWARDS, November 6, 1788. Robert Donoho,
surety. Consent of Joh Edwards, father of Elizabeth.

WILLIAM WATTS and ANN WRIGHT, July 23, 1792. Benjamin Watts, surety.
Consent of John Wright.

JAMES WARWICKE and ELIZABETH MARTIN, December 18, 1780. William Martin,
surety. Consent of Elizabeth herself.

JOHN WRIGHT and MARY HUNTER, December 28, 1789. Francis Hunter, surety.
Certificate of Mary saying she is of full age.

JAMES WILLIAMSON and DEBORAH MILAM, December 23, 1793. James Williamson,
surety. Consent of Elizabeth Milam.

SAMUEL WILSON and RUTH THURMAN, September 29, 1791. John Thurman, surety.
Certificate of Ruth that she is of full age.

JAMES WHITE and LUCY TERRY, February 13, 1783. John Mead, surety.
Consent of Thomas Terry, father of Lucy.

DANIEL WHITE and MARGARET CALDWELL, July 27, 1780. Thos. North, Jr.,
surety. Consent of Geo. Caldwell, the father of Margaret.

ROBERT WOODCOCK and ANNE HAILE, July 6, 1793. John Radford, surety.
Consent of Stephen and Nancey Haile, the parents of Anne.

JOSIAH WOOD and SUSANNA KARNS, July 25, 1797. John Dooley, surety.
Consent of Michal Karns, father of Susanna.

DOMINIE WELCH and MARY PARKER, October 21, 1785. James Pritchard, surety.
Consent of Mary herself.

JOHN WARREN and SARAH BELLAMY, February 27, 1799. Bury Bryant, surety.
Consents of Sarah, Samuel and Anea Bellamy.

ANTHONY WRIGHT and ELIZABETH MAYS, December 18, 1789. James Mays, surety.
Consent of John Wright, father of Anthony.

FRANCIS WRIGHT and SALLY HARDWICKE, September 9, 1794. Peter Hunter,
surety. Consent of Sally herself.

MILBURN WILLIAMSON and MILLEY COCKERHAM, April 12, 1788. Solomon Butler,
surety. Consent of John Williamson, father of Milburn; and of
Susanna Cockerham, mother of Milley.

JOHN WHARTON and SALLY LOGWOOD, May 29, 1797. Hardaway Hatcher, surety.
Consent of Thomas Logwood, father of Sally.

JNO. WARD, widower, and SARAH LYNCH, widow, December 27, 1766. Isham
Talbot, surety. Consent of Sarah herself.

WILLIAM WHEELER and SARAH WRIGHT, December 19, 1785. Rowland Wheeler,
surety. Certificate of Sarah that she is of age.

JESSE WILKS and FANEY GULDIN, January 8, 1799. Amson Metton, surety.
Certificate of Faney.

JOSEPH WILSON and POLLY THURMAN, January 14, 1795. George Welch, surety.
Consent of Joseph Wilson and Joseph Thurman.

BASIL WHEAT and FRANCES OVERSTREET, December 10, 1800. John Overstreet. Consent of James Overstreet, father of Frances.

ANDERSON WHEELER and SARAH NIMMO, June 5, 1787. Roland Wheeler, surety. Consent of Robert Nimmo, the father of Sarah.

BENJAMIN WATTS and MARY WRIGHT, December 21, 1786. Thomas Wright, surety. Consent of John Wright, father of Mary.

WILLIAM WALTON and MARY LEFTWICH, January 30, 1778. Robert Alexander, surety. Consent of W. Leftwich, father of Mary.

LEONARD WILLIAMSON and BETSEY WILSON, September 6, 1799. No surety given. Consent of James Willson, father of Betsey.

THOMAS WRIGHT and SALLEY PULLEN, March 26, 1792. John Wright, surety. Consent of Thomas Pullen, Senr., father of Salley.

DAVID WRIGHT and AMELIA HOWELL, March 4, 1797. John Howell, surety. Consent of David and Rebecka Howell, the parents of Amelia.

JOHN HENRY WOODROFF of Amherst County, and EMMY GATEWOOD, February 26, 1783. Thomas Gatewood, surety. Consent of James Gatewood, father of Emmy.

RANDOLPH WOODEY and PATIENCE MORGAN, November 19, 1792. John Woody, surety. Consent of Thomas and Susannah Morgin.

JOSHUA WADE and ANN BOATRIGHT, October 28, 1786. Thomas McLaughlin, surety. Consent of William Boatright.

MATTHEW WORLEY and RACHEL WHEAT, April 18, 1785. Caleb Tate, surety. Consent of John Wheate, father of Rachel.

EDWARD WOODHAM and WINIFRED TERRELL, November 26, 1781. Benjamin Arthur, surety. Consent of David Terrell, father of Winifred, saying she is 21 years old.

WILLIAM WHITE and CHARLOTTE CUNDIFF, May 16, 1792. Elisha Cundiff, surety. Consent of John and Lucy Whight.

JESSE WOOD and NANCY ROSSER, August 3, 1781. John Rosser, surety. Consent of Jonathan Rosser.

ANDERSON WOOD and MARGARET MEADOR, August 4, 1800. Allen Drake, surety. Consent of Thomas Meador, father of Margaret.

MEREDITH WRIGHT and LUCY GATEWOOD, December 12, 1794. John Murphy, Jr., surety. Consent of James Gatewood, father of Lucy.

JOHN WILLIAMSON and NANCY BLANKENSHIP, December 24, 1798. Drury Holland, surety. Certificate of Nancy herself.

EUCLID WILLS and BETSY STUART, April 3, 1780. David Irvine, surety. Consent of Elizabeth Smith, mother of Betsy.

GEORGE WIGGINTON and SISLEY REYNOLDS, December 22, 1788. Joseph Drury, surety. Consent of Sisley herself.

THOMAS WALKER and ANN HART, February 13, 1778. William Walker, surety. Consent of William Hart, father of Ann.

PIERCE WADE and ELIZABETH THURMOND, May 22, 1780. John Miller, surety. Consent of John Thurmond, father of Elizabeth.

JOHN WALKER and ELIZABETH BROWN, December 29, 1794. Thomas Andrews, surety. Consent of Elizabeth stating that she is of full age.

JOHN WEBSTER and MAGGY WALKER, June 28, 1779. John Merritt, surety. Consent of Richard Webster, father of John; and of James Walker, father of Maggy.

ZACKRIAH WHEAT and BETSEY KENEDY, December 9, 1791. Samuel Hatcher, surety. Consent of Easter Kenedy, mother of Betsey.

GEORGE WEST and SARAH JAMES, November 11, 1791. Daniel James, surety.

BENJAMIN WRIGHT and MARY WEEKES, February 29, 1796. William Wright, surety. Consent of John Wright, father of Benjamin.

SAMUEL WARNER and SARAH STIFF, April 25, 1778. James Stiff, surety.

DAVID WILSON and CATHARINE McCLENACHAN, November 13, 1779. Thomas McClenachan, surety.

DAVID WRIGHT, widower, and NANNY TURNER, widow, November 8, 1770. Robt. Ewings, surety.

WILLIAM WOMACK and RACHEL GILPIN, October 28, 1797. Francis G. Gilpin, surety.

JEREMIAH WADE and PEGGY WEEKES, December 20, 1800. Alderson Weekes, surety.

WILLIAM WEEKES and ELIZABETH FRANKLIN, September 5, 1797. John Witt, surety.

THOMAS WHITE and JANE LUSK, March 18, 1783. Araba Brown, surety.

LUKE WALLACE and HANNAH OLDAKER, May 19, 1795. John Oldaker, surety.

JEREMIAH WOOD and MARY DOOLEY, December 28, 1796. Peter Fitzhugh, surety. Consent of John Dooley, father of Mary.

DAVID WRIGHT and SARAH TALBOT, daughter of Isham Talbot, September 28, 1782. James Steptoe, surety.

CHARLES WILLIAMS and SUSANNA WILLIAMS, April 11, 1797. Roger Williams, surety.

JAMES WILLIAMSON and ELIZABETH HALL, June 28, 1773. Leonard Hall, surety.

ZACHARIAH WORLEY and LUCY KERR, June 13, 1785. Wm. Kerr, Jr., surety. Consent of William Kerr, father of Lucy.

SAMUEL WHITTAKER and MARY HARRIS, April 24, 1797. William Ingledue, surety.

THOMAS WILCOX and WINIFRED CAFFERY, May 8, 1778. Charles Caffery, surety.

JAMES WILLIAMSON and ELIZABETH MILAM, December ___, 1791. Aran Campbell, surety.

WILLIAM WILLS and FRANCES TYLER, January 12, 1791. William Boatright, surety.

JACOB WADE and MARY BRANCH, October 31, 1800. George Stone, surety.

SAMUEL WOODWARD and CELIA BROWN, October 21, 1779. John Consolver, surety. Edward Bright and Mary Ann Bright, grandparents of Celia.

WILLIAM WILLIAMS and SARAH TEWLEY, February 27, 1787. John Williams, surety. Consent of John Tewley, father of Sarah.

THOMAS WATKINS and MARY PETTIT, November 19, 1787. Thomas Pettit, surety. Consent of Lewis Pettit, father of Mary.

JAMES WILKERSON and SUCKEY HUMPHREY, September 29, 1795. Lewis Humphrey, surety. Consent of William Humphrey, father of Suckey.

ABRAHAM WHITWORTH and NANCY BOARD, January 9, 1799. Meredith Campbell, surety. Consent of Abaslum Board, father of Nancy.

WILLIAM WRIGHT and HULDAH PULLEN, January 28, 1792. John Edgar, surety. Consent of Thos. Pullen, father of Huldah.

MATTHEW WORLEY and ELIZABETH HILLEY, May 11, 1790. William Shepherd, surety. Consent of Elizabeth herself.

JOHN WILKERSON and SUSANNA JOHNSON, December 1, 1792. Thomas Markham, surety. Consent of John Johnson, father of Susanna.

JOSEPH WILKERSON and ELIZABETH BLAZEBROOK FOWLER, April 29, 1785. Rush Milam, surety. Consent of Elizabeth Fowler, mother of Elizabeth.

GEORGE WELCH and NANCY CANNADY, December 16, 1790. George Cannady, surety.

JOHN WILSON, batchelor, and ELIZABETH HUNTER, spinster, October 23, 1769. Samuel Hunter, surety.

JOHN WALDEN and PATSEY HOPKINS, April 5, 1786. Francis Hopkins, surety.

WILLIAM WHITTON and SARAH HALL, February 20, 1786. Leonard Hall, surety.

THOMAS WELCH and POLLY YOUNG, November 26, 1787. John Young, surety.

ROBERT WARMOCK and NANCEY HALLEY, June 15, 1799. Francis Halley, Jr., surety.

NATHANIEL WILSON and MARY HARRIS, November 7, 1796. Nathaniel Harris, surety.

MILLS WITT and BETHANI CREASEY, April 25, 1797. Thomas Creasey, surety.

ROBERT WITT and NANCY REECE, August 18, 1790. Isaac Wade, surety.

JAMES WILLIAMS and SALLEY DALLICE, December 22, 1795. Marmaduke Dallice, surety.

JOHN WILSON and SARAH HUNTER, December 12, 1799. Francis Hunter, surety.

WILLIAM WHITE and POLLY P. PRICE, April 5, 1799. Thomas Reid, surety.

GEORGE WILSON and NANCY THURMAN, October 8, 1789. Joseph Thurman, surety.

JOSHUA WILLIAMS and BETSEY FUQUA, January 9, 1799. Joseph Fuqua, surety. Consent of Anney Fuqua, mother of Betsey.

THOMAS WALROND and SALLY TATE, June 12, 1799. Jesse Tate, surety. Consent of Benja. Walrond, Sr., father of Thomas; and also consent of Sally herself.

DAVID WILLIAMS and ELIZABETH AYRES, November 29, 1786. Edward Hore and John Wilks, sureties. Consent of James Ayres, the father of Elizabeth.

JOHN WELCH and LUCY ROBERTSON, January 5, 1791. Thomas Carns, surety. Consent of Thomas Robertson, father of Lucy.

WILLIAM WRIGHT and ANN O'NEEL, March 26, 1788. David Douglas, surety. Consent of Ann herself, that she is of age.

JOHN WILKERSON and REBECCA OLDAKERS, June 9, 1792. Henry Oldakers, surety. Consent of John Oldakers, father of Rebecca.

OWEN WILKERSON and SARAH MARKUM (MARKHAM) February 17, 1787. Arthur Markum, surety. Consent of Joseph Wilkerson, father of Owen.

ELISHA WHITTON and JENNY GADDY, January 31, 1791. Joseph Gadde, surety. Consent of Sherwood Gadde, father of Jenny.

JAMES WILLSON and JUDEY BOOTH, February 28, 17780. John Booth, surety. Consent of Judey herself.

REASON WILLIAMS and MARY HALLEY, January 20, 1795. Giles Halley, surety. Consent of Mary, saying that she is of age.

THOMAS WILLIAMS and MARY CRANTZ, December 28, 1789. Solomon Butler, surety. Consent of Michael Krants, father of Mary.

ISRAEL WINFRY (WINFREE) and FANNY HALLEY, June 1, 1791. Robert Thomas, surety. Consent of Francis Halley, father of Fanny.

ASA WILSON and ELIZABETH COCKERALL, January 8, 1798. Moses Mayhew, surety. Consent of John Mayhugh and Elizabeth Corkall.

ISAAC WINFREY and SARAH STRATTON, March 28, 1787. John Stratton, surety.
Consent of Henry Stratton, the father of Sarah.

TOMMY WRIGHT and SYNTHIA MAYSE, December 15, 1785. William Halley, surety.
Consent of James Mayse.

JOHN WILKS and BARBERRY NUMAN, August 31, 1795. Edmond Franklin, surety.
Consent of Conrad Newman.

JESSE WITT and ALEY BROWN, May 6, 1786. Henry Brown, surety. Consent of
Aley, saying she is of age.

JOHN WIGINGTON and MARGET McGEORGE, September 5, 1787. Joseph Drury,
surety. Consent of Thomas Overstreet, hatter. Also consent
of Margit herself.

ISAAC WADE and MARY STEVENS, February 8, 1779. Alexander Gibbs, surety.
Consent of Robert _____.

ISAAC WRIGHT and NANCY GOFF, October 9, 1799. John Goff, Jr., surety.
Consent of Joseph Goff, father of Nancy.

GEORGE WHITE and ANNE DOWDY, November 1, 1800. Eusebius Stone, surety.
Consent of John and Mare Dowdy, parents.

THOMAS WRIGHT and CHARITY BALINGER HILTON, February 24, 1790. Benjamin
Watts, surety. Consent of Lucy Hilton.

ZACHARIAH WORLEY and MILLEY DEWITT, May 27, 1799. James Dewitt, surety.

WILLIAM WATSON and JOICE OWEN, January 23, 1797. William Owen, surety.

MICHAEL YOAKUM, batchelor and ANNE BOYLES, February 8, 1762. Alexr.
Boyles, surety.

WILLIAM YOUNG and SALLEY VAUGHAN, July 6, 1793. John Young, surety.
Consent of Salley Van, herself, saying she is of age.

DUNCAN YOUNG and ANN LEWIS, September 4, 1790. Joseph Tyler, surety.
Consent of Ann, saying she is of age.

Hore, Mary 65
Howard, Delpha 24
　Mary 49
　Nancy 40
Howell, Amelia 73
　Elizabeth 21, 34
　Frankey 34
　Mackaria 11
　Patsey 4
　Polley 9
Howerton, Elizabeth 63
Hubbard, Betsy 23
Huddleston, Elizabeth 21
　Mary 61
　Nancey 67
　Rachel 31
　Sarah 3
Hudnall, Frankey 1
　Joannah 66
　Mary 33
Hughes, Elizabeth R. 52
　Delphia 64
　Lucy Gardner 23
　Mary 47
　Sally 33
Humphrey, Suckey 75
Hunt, Chizia 53
　Ohizia 53
　Polly 41
Hunter, Elizabeth 47, 75
　Mary 72
　Nancy 44, 49
　Sarah 76
Hurt, Mille 23
　Obedience 17
　Ruth 52
　Sally 53
　Tempe 13
Huston, Mary 47
Hutson, Patty 64
Hylton, Lucy 69

-I-

Inman, Polly 42
　Sarah 48
Irvin, Margaret 44
Irvine, Betsey 58
　Elizabeth 12, 70
　Margaret 62
　Mary 1, 46
　Nancy 44
　Sarah 7

-J-

Jackson, Ann 36
　Betsey 32
　Eleanor 67
　Hannah Cobb 36
　Jemima 18
　Patience 9
James, Eve 28
　Polly 36
　Sarah 74
Jarred, Rachel 52
Jarrel, Amy 60
Jarvis, Nancy 27
Jennings, Ann 9
　Mary 54
Jeter, Jency 42
　Nancy 55

Johnson, Agness 13, 37
　Elizabeth 30
　Judith 67
　Mary 18, 47
　Mourning 69
　Phebe 51
　Salley 6
　Susanna 47, 75
Johnston, Molly, 67
Jones, Agness 41
　Ann 25
　Elizabeth 2, 5
　Fanny 6
　Jemima 25
　Jenny 21
　Lucy 70
　Mary 4, 42
　Nancy 11
　Peggy 5
Jordan, Lucy 5
　Roseanna 18

-K-

Karn, Elizabeth 11
Karns, Susanna 72
Kasey, Ann 65
　Mary 46
Keeth, Nancy 19
Kelly, Evey 63
Kenedy, Betsey 74
Kennedy, Izbell 38
　Julia 34
　Rebeckah 1
Kennett, Mary 68
Kern, Barbara 39
　Hannah 39
Kerns, Anna 64
Kerr, Lucy 74
Key, Judith 48
　Milley 68
　Winney Caudle 9
King,Elizabeth 71
　Nancy 39
　Sally 53
　Theodotia 20
Kinzer, Cathrine 23

-L-

Lambert, Dinah 15
Langsdon, Lucy 47
Lazenby, Keziah 27
Lee, Rebecca 40
Leftwich, Charlotte 15
　Elizabeth 9, 63
　Emelia 1
　Lockey 65
　Mary 20, 73
　Mildred 51
　Polly 48
　Sally 69
Lemert, Mary 34
Lewis, Ann 77
Logwood, Martha Hill 7
　Nancy 66
　Sally 72
Low, Anne 26
Lowry, Elizabeth 15, 40
Loyd, Katy 46
　Patty 31
　Sarah 64
Luellin, Susannah 43

Lumpkin, Sophia 5
Lusk, Jane 74
Lynch, Elizabeth 51
　Sarah 72

-Mc-

McCan, Mary 36
　Sally 12
McCargo, Kitty Miller 71
McCartee, Febey 11
McClanahan, Martha 38
　Mary 11
　Rachell 16
McClard, Mary 19
McClenachan, Catharine 74
McCormack, Elizabeth 5
McCoy, Elizabeth 11
　Margaret 54
　Mary 50
　Sarah 11
McDonald, Rachel 17
McElwaine, Jane 1
McGeorge, Elizabeth 61
　Marget 77
McGhee, Betsey 5
McGlothlan, Nancy 18
McGlothlen, Mary 51
McGuire, Mary 62
McNob, Sarah 3
McNod, Sarah 3

-M-

Magers, Nancy 27
Major, Frances 24
Mann, Elizabeth 28
　Mary 14
　Nancy 69
　Rachel 56
Markum, Sarah 76
Marshall, Michael 7
Martin, Elizabeth 60, 72
　Fanny 22
　Frances 70
　Mary 22
　Nancy 56
　Rachel 64
Mason, Elizabeth 38
　Rhoda 22
　Sally 58
Mastin, Elizabeth 28
　Jenny 8
Maxey, Suckey 31
Mayberry, Elizabeth 38
　Kathrine 9
　Molly 25
Mays, Elizabeth 35, 72
　Frankey 16
　Nancy 6
Mayse, Salley 7
　Synthia 77
Meador, Fanny 17
　Margaret 73
　Mary 43
Meadow, Sarah 29
Meridy, Polley 60
Merritt, Clary 12
　Elizabeth 53
　Rhoda 44
Middleton, Mary 53
Mikle, Mary 64

BEDFORD COUNTY, VIRGINIA

INDEX OF WILLS

From 1754 to 1830

Edited by
ROWLAND D. BUFORD
Late Clerk of Bedford Co., Va.

BEDFORD COUNTY, VIRGINIA
Index to Wills
1754 to 1830

**The name of the testator is followed by the date of the probate of the will

A

Abston, Jesse, 26 March, 1822.
Adams, John, 23 January, 1797.
Adams, John, 25 November, 1824.
Allen, Reynolds, 25 October, 1779.
Allen, Robert, 22 March, 1773.
Allford, Silvator, 24 November, 1777.
Anderson, Elizabeth, 22 April, 1799.
Anderson, George, 25 May, 1778.
Anderson, Jacob, 23 December, 1822.
Anderson, Nelson, 28 August, 1820.
Anthony, John, 24 November, 1760.
Arthur, Barnabas, 26 July, 1815.
Arthur, John, 28 January, 1793.
Arthur, Thomas, 24 January, 1820.
Asbury, James, 24 September, 1827.
Aunspaugh, Catharine, 27 March, 1820.
Austin, Esther, 25 March, 1816.
Austin, Robert, 27 March, 1809.
Austin, William, 23 February, 1801.
Ayres, Hannah, 24 December, 1810.
Ayres, James, Sr., 24 July, 1797.

B

Baber, William, 27 February, 1809.
Ballard, William, 29 April, 1794.
Ballard, William, 24 February, 1817.
Banester, Isaac, 24 January, 1803.
Banister, William, 28 April, 1767.
Banks, Thomas, 23 September, 1755.
Bates, John, 22 December, 1777.
Bayne, George, 12 April, 1825.
Beard, Adam, 23 March, 1778.
Beard, Adam, 25 February, 1788.
Beard, Elizabeth, 23 March, 1778.
Beard, John, 26 November, 1780.
Beard, John, Sr., 24 September, 1787.
Bellamy, Samuel, 22 April, 1822.
Bennett, Peter, 25 May, 1778.
Birdwell, George, 26 November, 1781.
Board, John Sr., 27 November, 1821
Bobbitt, Lucy, 27 October, 1788.
Bodecker, William, 27 February, 1770.
Bond, Isaac, 26 January, 1824.

Bowles, Henry, 27 August, 1821.
Bowles, Jane, 25 March, 1816.
Bowles, John, 23 November, 1812.
Bowyer, Frederick, 22 December, 1777.
Boyd, William, 23 March, 1761.
Boyd, William, 27 January, 1794.
Bramblett, James, 27 November, 1758.
Bramblitt, William, 23 August, 1779.
Brander, Rev. John, 28 July, 1778.
Brickey, Jarret, 25 October, 1790.
Bright, Charles, 23 August, 1819.
Bright, Edward, 25 October, 1784.
Bright, Joseph, 26 July, 1819.
Brooke, Elizabeth, 22 February, 1802.
Brown, Daniel, Sr., 27 February, 1797.
Brown, Henry, 24 June, 1799.
Brown, James, 26 July, 1790.
Brown, John, 23 March, 1778.
Brown, Joseph, 26 October, 1795.
Bruer, Richard, 25 September, 1804.
Bryan, William, 28 February, 1764.
Buford, Henry, 23 January, 1815.
Buford, Thomas, 28 November, 1774.
Bunch, James, 27 September, 1802.
Burgess, William, 27 July, 1778.
Burton, Robert, 22 February, 1819.
Burton, William, 25 February, 1811.
Bush, John, 24 January, 1774.
Butler, William, 27 October, 1794.

C

Callaway, George, 25 January, 1773.
Callaway, James, 27 November, 1809.
Callaway, Mary, 28 January, 1822.
Callaway, William, Sr., 24 September, 1821.
Campbell, Moses, 23 April, 1792.
Campbell, William, 22 January, 1781.
Candler, Daniel, 27 May, 1766.
Cannada, William, 28 February, 1791.
Cantrell, Sarah, 22 March, 1784.
Carson, John, 25 May, 1762.
Chaffin, Joseph, 22 June, 1812.
Chaffin, Joshua, 26 July, 1813.
Chastain, John, 28 September, 1807.
Cheatwood, John, 24 November, 1828.
Chiles, Henry, 24 April, 1758.
Clark, Mary Ann, 25 November, 1828.
Clarke, Isham, 23 August, 1824.
Clay, Charles, Rev., 27 March, 1820.
Cofer, Josias, 22 August, 1814.
Coleman, James, 24 September, 1815.
Connelly, James, 28 August, 1780.

Cook, Andrew, 27 July, 1778.
Corley, Caniel, 22 June, 1807.
Cowan, Elizabeth, 27 May, 1816.
Cowan, Elizabeth, 26 August, 1816. (Codicil)
Cowan, Robert, 25 April, 1803.
Cox, Valentine, 27 December, 1812. (not proved)
Creasey, John, Sr., 28 November, 1825.
Credell, Humphrey, 22 May, 1780.
Creesey, Thomas, 25 July, 1803.
Creesey, William, 28 September, 1812.
Crump, Susanna, 27 January, 1812.

D

Dabney, Cornelius, 22 October, 1792.
Dale, Frances, 28 July, 1777.
Daugherty, Hugh, 22 September, 1788.
Daulton, Timothy, 24 April, 1775.
Davis, Samuel, 26 February, 1798.
Davis, Zachary, 27 June, 1791.
Deardorff, Peter, 28 October, 1816.
DeWitt, James, 27 September, 1824.
Dickinson, Joseph, 28 September, 1818.
Dillard, Thomas, 28 August, 1820.
Dixon, Thomas, 27 February, 1770.
Dixon, William, 23 October, 1809.
Dobyns, Griffin, 27 December, 1819.
Dollard, Reuben, 25 June, 1804.
Donald, Andrew, 29 May, 1806.
Donald, Lucy, 24 July, 1809.
Dooley, Thomas, 22 June, 1778.
Dooley, Thomas, 22 September, 1823.
Douglass, George, 24 November, 1812.
Dowdy, John, 28 July, 1806.
Dowell, Francis, 22 March, 1819.
Downing, John, 22 December, 1777.

E

Earley, Joshua, 28 December, 1812.
Early, Jeremiah, 27 September, 1779.
Eckhols, John, 22 June, 1795.
Edgars, George, 22 October, 1765.
Edwards, William, 23 May, 1757.
Eidson, Boyce, 25 March, 1816.
Embree, Moses, 26 April, 1796.
English, Stephen, 24 March, 1783.
Erwin or Irvine, Joseph, 26 October, 1818.
Estes, Benjamin, 22 July, 1816.

Estes, John H. T., 29 March, 1816.
Everitt, Simmonds, 25 November, 1822.
Ewing, Charles, 24 July, 1770.
Ewing, Robert, 25 June, 1787.
Ewing, William, 23 April, 1810.

F

Feazel, Philip, 26 October, 1789.
Ferguson, Jeremiah, 26 January, 1829.
Ferguson, John, 25 September, 1786.
Ferrell, William, 23 October, 1780.
Field, John, 26 May, 1823.
Fields, John, 27 July, 1778.
Floyd, James, 13 September, 1826.
Franklin, Mary Ann, 27 October, 1794.
Fuqua, John, 26 September, 1796.
Fuqua, Joseph, 22 June, 1829.
Fuqua, Ralph, 24 July, 1770.
Fuqua, Thomas, 22 December, 1806.

G

Gadde, Shearwood, 26 September, 1803.
Gaddy, Ann, 28 October, 1816.
Gaddy, Bartholomew, 28 October, 1822.
Gaddy, George, 26 September, 1785.
Gibson, James, 26 February, 1765.
Gibson, William, 27 August, 1792.
Gilbert, Samuel, 28 October, 1776.
Gilliam, Richard, 22 April, 1799.
Gilpin, Francis G., 27 March, 1826.
Goad, John, 23 July, 1771.
Goff, Joseph, 28 December, 1828.
Goode, John, 24 July, 1775.
Gouldman, Edward, 24 December, 1774.
Gower, Stanley, 23 December, 1782.
Gray, John, 28 March, 1786.
Gray, Sarah, 27 September, 1802.
Green, Edward, 26 September, 1825.
Green, John, 24 July, 1775.
Greer, Joseph, 28 May, 1781.
Griffith, George, 25 August, 1777.
Gwatkin, James, 28 February, 1820.

H

Hackworth, Joseph, 23 June, 1823.
Hail, Richard, 28 June, 1784.
Haile, Francis, 28 August, 1780.
Hairston, Peter, 27 March, 1780.
Hall, Hezekiah, 22 July, 1811.
Hall, John, 22 September, 1794.

92

Halley, Francis, 23 August, 1813.
Halley, Henry, 24 February, 1800.
Halley, John, 27 December, 1802.
Hamilton, Thomas, 28 September, 1772.
Hancock, George, 27 January, 1783. (of S. Car.)
Hancock, Simon, 24 January, 1791.
Hardwick, Robert, 28 June, 1784.
Hardy, Robert, 28 January, 1828.
Hardy, Solomon, 25 May, 1825.
Harris, Charles, 27 November, 1815.
Harrison, Elisha, 27 July, 1812.
Hatcher, Deme, 28 October, 1816.
Hatcher, Edward, 28 January, 1782.
Hatcher, Hardaway, 30 May, 1822.
Hatcher, Henry, 22 December, 1800.
Hatcher, Jeremiah, 23 July, 1804.
Hatcher, Jeremiah, Jr., 27 May, 1816.
Hatcher, Julius, 28 September, 1807.
Hatcher, Reuben, 28 June, 1790.
Haynes, Henry, 25 November, 1816.
Haynes, William, 25 June, 1781.
Haynes, Thomas, 24 February, 1806.
Hayth, William, 24 April, 1775.
Headen, William, 25 May, 1818.
Hilton, James, 25 September, 1786.
Hix, James, 26 July, 1813.
Hix, Rebecca, 27 May, 1822.
Hix, William, 24 August, 1812.
Hoard, William, 28 August, 1781.
Hobson, Benjamin, 28 October, 1817.
Hogan, Obadiah, 27 April, 1818.
Hole, Charles, 23 January, 1804.
Holladay, John, 28 December, 1812.
Holligan, John, 23 November, 1772.
Holt, Rev. John White, 27 September, 1790.
Holt, Joseph, Sr., 23 September, 1805.
Hopkins, Francis, 25 June, 1804.
Horn, George, 29 March, 1825.
Hubbard, John, 26 July, 1824.
Huddleston, Abraham, 28 November, 1785.
Hudnall, William, 22 February, 1813.
Hudson, Joel, 28 January, 1811.
Hunter, Alexander, 22 March, 1768.
Hurt, Moses, 28 July, 1806.

I

Irvine, Christopher, 26 July, 1769.
Irvine, William, 25 February, 1767.
Irvine, William, 22 June, 1829.

J

Jackson, Jervis, 28 June, 1802.
James, William, 27 July, 1807.
Jeter, Henry, 24 September, 1821.
Johnson, Benjamin, 26 September, 1769.
Johnson, David, 25 September, 1809.
Johnson, John, 25 August, 1817.
Johnson, Timothy, 28 December, 1801.
Jones, James C., 22 November, 1824.
Jones, Michael, 22 January, 1781.
Jones, Stephen, Jr., 25 August, 1828.
Jones, William, 28 May, 1781.
Jones, William, 30 May, 1816.
Jordan, Absalom, 22 May, 1826.

K

Kannady, George, 27 February, 1815.
Kasey, James, 28 October, 1816.
Kennedy, John, 24 September, 1781.
Kennon, Kitturah, 26 July, 1813.
Kern, Michael, 23 February, 1807.
Kerr, William, 27 June, 1791.
Kesson, David, 27 Nov. 1820.
Keshman, Martin, 24 September, 1804.
Krantz, Abraham, 25 March, 1813.
Krantz, Michael, 26 April, 1802.

L

Lainhart, John Christopher, 27 September, 1779.
Lambert, Charles, 24 December, 1798.
Lamont, John, 27 October, 1823.
Latham, Henry, 23 May, 1808.
Lawson, Jonas, 24 September, 1771.
Lee, Richard, 24 April, 1815.
Lee, Tabitha, 28 July, 1828.
Lee, William, 26 September, 1803.
Leftwich, Augustine, 22 June, 1795.
Leftwich, Littlebury, 23 June, 1823.
Leftwich, Thomas, 24 June, 1816.
Leftwich, William, Sr., 26 June, 1820.
Lewellan, Mary, 23 May, 1826.
Lewis, John, 25 February, 1805.
Linn, Adam, 24 March, 1772.
Lockett, Mary, 23 September, 1805.
Logwood, Martha, 26 May, 1822.
Logwood, Thomas, 24 September, 1821.
Loving, William, 22 September, 1767.

M

McCormack, William, 23 October, 1775.
McCraw, Edward, 25 September, 1820.
McCraw, Mary, 23 August, 1824.
McGeorge, Lawrence, 26 August, 1828.
McGlothlan, John, 27 December, 1813.
McIlheny, Thomas, 27 January, 1777.
McMurtree, James, 24 March, 1772.
Maples, Richard, 28 February, 1774.
Markle, Charles, Sr., 28 April, 1828.
Mars, John, 28 April, 1806.
Marshall, Thomas, 25 October, 1819.
Martin, Robert, 28 May, 1781.
Mayberry, Frederick, 26 October, 1801.
Mays, James, 22 June, 1795.
Mayse, John, 26 November, 1821.
Meador, Ambrose, 28 September, 1795.
Meador, Jeremiah, Sr., 27 January, 1817.
Meador, John, 23 January, 1826.
Melton, Absalom, 23 September, 1805.
Meriwether, Catharine, E. 26 November, 1827.
Merritt, Thomas, 25 June, 1810.
Messon, David, 27 November, 1820.
Metcalfe, Vernon, 26 January, 1818.
Milam, Benjamin, 22 October, 1781.
Milam, Sally, 24 November, 1828.
Milam, Thomas, 27 March, 1775.
Miller, John, 26 July, 1785.
Miller, Simon, 28 February, 1785.
Millner, William, 27 November, 1820.
Mitchell, Daniel, 25 September, 1775.
Mitchell, Robert, 25 February, 1799.
Moody, William, 22 June, 1795.
Moon, Jacob, Jr., 28 May, 1781.
Moon, Jesse, 23 October, 1780.
Moore, Thomas, 27 March, 1826.
Moorman, Silas, 24 February, 1777.
Moorman, Thomas, 25 November, 1766.
Morlan, Stephen, 22 October, 1810.
Morgan, Morgan, 28 July, 1828.
Morgan, Samuel, 26 June, 1815.
Morgan, Thomas, 23 May, 1774.
Morris, Ambrose, Sr., 29 November, 1826.
Morris, Daniel, 24 November, 1767.
Morris, Tabithy, 24 August, 1778.
Murphy, John, Sr., 25 October, 1819.
Murphy, Thomas, 22 June, 1778.
Myers, Elizabeth, 26 June, 1826.
Myler, Matthew, 24 August, 1818.

N

Neal, Daniel, 25 April, 1803.
Neal, John, 25 March, 1818.
Nelms, Presley, 25 June, 1804.
Nichols, George, Sr., 24 February, 1812.
Nichols, John, 26 December, 1803.
Nimmo, Robert, Sr., 28 January, 1822.
Noell, Cornelius, Sr., 27 March, 1821.
Noell, Jesse, 27 November, 1821.
North, Abraham, 28 April, 1800.

O

Oglesby, Richard, 26 August, 1811.
Oglesby, Sarah, Sr., 26 June, 1780.
Otey, John, 24 March, 1817.
Overstreet, Thomas, Sr., 27 February, 1792.
Owen, James, 26 November, 1827.

P

Palmore, Benjamin, 26 September, 1825.
Palmore, John, 22 August, 1825.
Pate, Edward, 24 May, 1768.
Pate, John, 23 September, 1767.
Patterson, Joseph, 23 September, 1811.
Payne, Archer, Jr., 22 September, 1806.
Payne, Flail, 26 July, 1784.
Payne, John, 22 October, 1798.
Pegram, Thomas, 28 December, 1818.
Phelps, John, 25 February, 1772.
Phelps, John, 28 September, 1801.
Phillips, Stephen, 25 February, 1788.
Pollard, Francis, 23 July, 1771.
Powell, Thomas, 26 August, 1822.
Prather, James, 27 June, 1759.
Prathor, Jonathan, 22 June, 1772.
Preston, John, 28 November, 1814.
Preston, Mary, 26 February, 1810.
Preston, Thomas, 26 February, 1798.
Price, Robert, 24 June, 1816.
Pryor, Harris, 27 February, 1804.
Pullen, Moses, 28 June, 1790.

Q

Quarles, Anna Maria, 28 December, 1829.
Quarles, John, 24 December, 1810.
Quarles, Sarah, 28 January, 1822.

R

Ramsey, Bartholomew, 25 February, 1793.
Rawlings, Benjamin, 23 June, 1777.
Ray, Joseph, 26 May, 1767.
Read, Francis, 25 October, 1819.
Read, John, 24 May, 1773.
Read, William, 24 September, 1798.
Rector, Jacob, 22 November, 1779.
Rentfro, Joseph, 25 March, 1776.
Reynolds, Jonas, 25 June, 1793.
Rice, Benjamin, 27 November, 1827.
Rice, Mary, 22 August, 1814.
Richardson, Jonathan, 24 May, 1773.
Richardson, Randolph, 28 October, 1782.
Roberts, Daniel, 22 October, 1781.
Roberts, Thomas, 26 March, 1781.
Robinson, James, 27 July, 1778.
Rogers, William, 26 March, 1759.
Rosebrough, Robert, 27 July, 1801.
Ross, John, Sr., 24 November, 1823.
Routon, Richard, 27 February, 1792.
Rowland, Henry, 23 August, 1773.
Roy, Peter, 28 March, 1815.
Rucker, Ambrose, 27 August, 1827.
Rusher, Andrew, 25 November, 1822.
Rust, George, 23 October, 1775.

S

Salmon, John, 24 January, 1791.
Scott, William, 24 November, 1794.
Scruggs, Gross, 28 July, 1788.
Scruggs, Thomas, 22 October, 1804.
Shands, William, 22 August, 1814.
Shaw, John, 24 July, 1786.
Sherman, Henry D., 28 March, 1814.
Sinkler, Robert, 23 July, 1827.
Skillern, Hannah B., 24 November, 1817.
Slinker, Christopher, 26 January, 1795.
Smelser, Paulser, 27 July, 1778.
Smith, Bowker, 28 March, 1768.
Smith, Guy, 24 September, 1781.
Snow, Thomas, 28 August, 1781.
Spradling, Benjamin, 27 September, 1819.
Spradling, Mary, 27 July, 1818.
St. Clair, Isaac, 22 June, 1829.
Staton, Thomas, 23 March, 1778.
Stemson, Martin, 24 May, 1768.
Steptoe, James, 27 February, 1826.
Steptoe, James C., 27 November, 1827.
Stewart, James, 24 August, 1784.
Stockton, William, 26 October, 1795.

Stone, Micajah, 24 June, 1799.
Stovall, John, 22 June, 1778.
Stratton, Henry, 23 December, 1799.
Stump, John, 23 July, 1787.
Sutton, Christopher, 26 January, 1807.

T

Talbot, Charles, 23 August, 1779.
Talbot, Matthew, 27 November, 1758.
Tanner, Michael, 26 May, 1777.
Tanner, Nathaniel, 22 July, 1782.
Tate, Charles, 24 December, 1792.
Tate, Jesse, 22 April, 1805.
Taylor, Henry, 25 August, 1777.
Taylor, Isaac, 23 February, 1778.
Taylor, James, 26 September, 1808.
Terry, William, 28 March, 1814.
Thomson, John, 25 May, 1778.
Thomson, Waddy, 1 June, 1827.
Thomson, William, 24 May, 1763.
Thornhill, William, 23 September, 1793.
Tracy, Micajah, 27 May, 1811.
Tracy, William, 28 December, 1812.
Trigg, William, 22 February, 1773.
Trueman, William, 23 January, 1797.
Truman, James, 28 July, 1828.
Turner, Admire, 28 September, 1818.
Turner, Elijah, Sr., 23 October, 1820.
Turner, Richard, 27 June, 1769.
Turpin, Thomas, 23 May, 1826.
Tyler, Mary, 25 April, 1825.

U

Uhle, Michael, 28 February, 1791.

V

Vaughan, Robert, 26 August, 1816.

W

Wade, Isaac, Sr., 22 September, 1823.
Wade, Jeremiah, 28 September, 1772.
Walker, Mary, 25 December, 1820.
Walker, Robert, 24 March, 1767.
Walker, Robert M., 24 July, 1827.
Ward, John, 23 December, 1782.
Watkins, Thomas, 26 July, 1773.
Watson, Johnson, 27 July, 1801.
Watts, Edward, 27 April, 1795.
Weeks, Alderson, Rev., 27 February, 1809.

Welch, Nicholas, 26 July, 1768.
Wells, Martin, 26 March, 1821.
West, Margaret, 22 July, 1822.
Wheeler, Thomas, 28 July, 1828.
White, Elizabeth, 24 September, 1827.
White, Henry, 27 September, 1802.
White, James, 28 July, 1828.
Whitehead, Joseph, 24 February, 1778.
Whitely, William, 30 March, 1821.
Wildman, William, 23 September, 1805.
Wilkerson, Joseph, 27 May, 1829.
Williams, John, 24 February, 1823.
Williamson, John, 23 February, 1801.
Williamson, John, 22 February, 1808.
Wilson, John, 26 November, 1780.
Wilson, Matthew, 26 March, 1771.
Wimmer, John, 23 October, 1789.
Witt, Anne, 28 October, 1816.
Womack, Jesse, 26 August, 1782.
Wood, Milly, 26 December, 1814.
Wood, Thomas, 25 February, 1793.
Woodward, Richard, 24 April, 1786.
Wooster, Hinmon, 27 February, 1797.
Worley, Francis, 26 November, 1780.
Worley, William, 22 October, 1787.
Wright, John, 26 September, 1803.
Wright, John, 25 June, 1810.
Wright, John, 25 December, 1814.
Wright, Joseph, 11 September, 1815.
Wright, Thomas, 22 November, 1763.

Y

Young, James, 25 May, 1778.

evelyn & Wilburn

Jha

4 4 4

$$275 \times 3 = 825$$

825
195
590

60
60
120
75
45
120
75
195
200
95

CPSIA information can be obtained at www.ICGtesting.com
Printed in the USA
BVOW031222091211

277943BV00005B/38/P